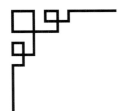
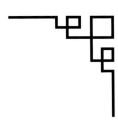

This text has been developed with the intermediate level signer in mind. The activities are designed to bring the student out of the structured classroom environment and into more natural communication situations. Students are provided with opportunities to explore a variety of registers and linguistic devices as they move toward communication competence in signed language.

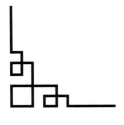
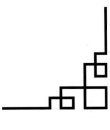

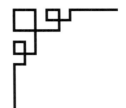

MEETING HALFWAY IN AMERICAN SIGN LANGUAGE

A Common Ground for Effective Communication
Among Deaf and Hearing People

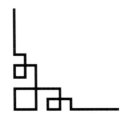

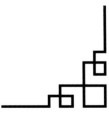

MEETING HALFWAY IN AMERICAN SIGN LANGUAGE

A Common Ground for Effective Communication
Among Deaf and Hearing People

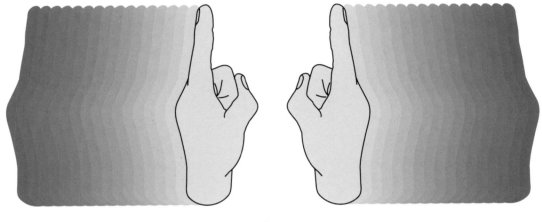

by

Bernard Bragg   and   Jack R. Olson

Photography by Denise Kyle Stenzel

Edited by Donald F. Moores
With a Foreword by Merv Garretson

Deaf Life Press
a division of MSM Productions, Ltd.
Rochester, New York
1994

Meeting Halfway in American Sign Language: A Common Ground for Effective Communication Among Deaf and Hearing People

Cover Design: Tony Landon McGregor
Layout and Formatting: Matthew S. Moore and Charles F. Bancroft

The authors and publisher wish to express their thanks to the publishers and poets who have given us permission to include the following poems in the exercise portion of the text:

Nick Beilenson, President, Peter Pauper Press, for the three haikus by Basho, Joso, and Masahide (p. 140). Reprinted by permission.

Doubleday Publishing Company for two haikus by Saigyo and Sanetomo and three by Tamekane (p. 140), originally published in **From the Country of Eight Islands: An Anthology of Japanese Poetry** by Hiroaki Sato and Burton Watson (Garden City, New York: Doubleday Anchor, 1981). Reprinted by permission.

William Morrow and Co., Inc., "Beauty" by E-Yeh-Shure (p. 143), from **I Am a Pueblo Girl**. Copyright © 1939. Reprinted by permission.

Holt Rinehart and Winston, "The Road Not Taken" by Robert Frost (p. 142), from **The Poetry of Robert Frost**, edited by Edward Connery Lathen. Copyright © 1916, © 1969 by Holt, Rinehart and Winston. Copyright © 1944 by Robert Frost. Reprinted by permission.

Alfred A. Knopf, Inc., for "Lenox Avenue Mural/Harlem" ["Dream Deferred"] by Langston Hughes (p. 143), from **The Panther and the Lash** by Langston Hughes. Copyright © 1951 by Langston Hughes. Reprinted by permission of Alfred A. Knopf, Inc.

David C. Berry for "On Reading Poems to a Senior Class at South High" (p. 141). Copyright © 1994 by D. C. Berry. Reprinted by permission of the author.

Cataloging-in-Publication Data
Bragg, Bernard, 1928-
Olson, Jack R., 1938-

Meeting Halfway in American Sign Language: A Common Ground for Effective Communication Among Deaf and Hearing People. By Bernard Bragg and Jack R. Olson. Photography by Denise Stenzel. Edited by Donald F. Moores. With a foreword by Merv Garretson.

Bibliography: p.
ISBN: 0-9634016-7-X (hardcover)
4. Sign language 2. Deaf—Culture. 3. Deaf studies. I. Title.

93-090674

Printed in the United States of America

The paper use in this publication meets the minimum requirements of American National Standard for Information Sciences—Permanence of Paper for Printed Library Materials, ANSI Z39.48-1984 (∞)

10 9 8 7 6 5 4 3 2
First Edition

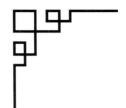
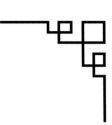

This book is dedicated to Robert F. Panara who is, in the eyes of many,
a shining model for clear communication in the Sign Language.

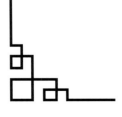
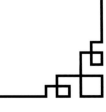

TABLE OF CONTENTS

Exercises

Practice Stories

ACKNOWLEDGMENTS

We are fully aware that in an undertaking such as this, literally hundreds of friends and colleagues contribute directly and indirectly to our work. This is in the form of knowledge, insights and perspectives that have been shared with us over the years, as well as comments and suggestions specifically related to the book and reactions to the materials in various draft forms.

It would be impossible to name all of the contributors, and we hesitate to do so because of the danger that we might inadvertently omit some of our more important sources of information and inspiration. However, twelve individuals deserve special thanks and public acknowledgement for their direct contributions to this book. In alphabetical order, they are:

Howard Busby
Kathee Christensen
Harvey Corson
Anne Feiler
Debbie Fenlason
Rachel Jaffee

Chun Louie
William Newell
Roslyn Rosen
Martin Sternberg
Jill Tieman
Ann Topliff

We would also like to acknowledge the following individuals who have contributed to the success of this book with their proofreading skills:

Carol Beckman
Mary Ken Chandler
Rob R. Hunt
Stacy Necessary Juhnke
Linda J. Levitan

FOREWORD

In this unique new book, **Meeting Halfway**, Bernard Bragg and Jack Olson have produced a series of lessons based on a refreshing and realistic perception of what actually happens in day-to-day communication among deaf and hearing people, as well as among deaf people themselves. I believe they recognize quite correctly that communication is not a rigid science, but rather a gentle art.

For some time now, I have been a bit disturbed by what I perceive to be a tendency to mix research with proselytizing among advocates of the different forms of sign communication. Language should not be forced on other people; it is simply one of the many ways people share their thoughts and feelings with each other. Communication needs to be natural and comfortable for each individual involved.

When I look back at my early childhood and adolescent years and recall the cruel oppression of signs, I can certainly empathize with deaf people and our hearing supporters who have been lashing back at oralism and a narrow insistence on English only. However, many of our advocates need to be reminded that it was not just ASL that was chained to the back alleys and bathrooms, but all forms of signing and fingerspelling, all manual communication.

ASL had not yet been analyzed by Bill Stokoe, although deaf Americans were using the language extensively and very frequently in the form described in this book. As a matter of fact, every time I see myself on videotape and observe carefully the signs of my many other deaf friends and colleagues, I have the feeling this book best describes our way of communicating in signs.

Both Bragg and Olson have been heavily committed to the world of communication arts for many years. Both have been involved in theatre work. Bragg is a world renowned actor, mime, director, author, and consultant. Olson presents an interesting intermix of sign, speech pathology, and audiology. Both have had extensive experience in teaching deaf children and youth, and others as well.

Englished ASL, the term used by the authors, may be what was in the past characterized as Pidgin Sign English (PSE). However, this type of communication is not pidgin but a unique way of communicating in a mixture of two wonderful languages. True ASL/English bilinguals actually sign this way, as well as in strictly ASL, which can be quicker and more visual and descriptive.

So, communication, rather than language, may be the basic focus of this book. Should a language, any language, not communicate with the person one is trying to reach, the language choice becomes a poor, impoverished mechanism for sharing thoughts, feelings, beliefs, and information. People not skilled at compromise and accommodation have lost the possibility for direct, personal communication.

The more options we have for casual, social, and professional interchange through different languages, the richer our quality of life. People who know more than one language have that many more roads open for information sharing, cultural enrichment, and simply the satisfaction of mind meeting mind. Obviously we cannot underestimate the impact of ASL and English upon each other. Any time two languages coexist in proximity we can expect borrowings, influences, and mutations. The 14th century English of Chaucer's day is certainly vastly different from the English we know today. Live languages are dynamic, not static. They change and they evolve.

I would hope that this new book will make people more aware of the vital need to "do what comes naturally" and not to have a hangup over which language or system is being used so long as there is clear communication. I think we need this breath of fresh air upon the communication scene as it relates to deaf people everywhere. It just might lead to a resolution of ongoing controversy among some over-technical linguists who need to understand that the rules and restrictions for delivering messages through a spoken language do not all apply to an entirely different mode of using language to communicate — not through speech but with the hands. In this country, both ASL and English belong to each other. True fluency in these languages can be achieved only by using them constantly, day to day, socially, in meetings, or wherever, flexibly, of course, as guided by each changing occasion.

— Merv Garretson

ABOUT THE AUTHORS

The authors of this text come from diverse and rich backgrounds. An accomplished actor, director, playwright and lecturer, Bernard Bragg was born deaf into a deaf family. He grew up in the world of theatre and has performed all his life for deaf and hearing audiences around the world. He attended the New York School for the Deaf, is a graduate of Gallaudet University, and holds a master's degree from San Francisco State University in Special Education with a minor in Drama. He taught at the California School for the Deaf in Berkeley. He studied with the world-renowned mime, Marcel Marceau, in Paris. He went on to help found the internationally acclaimed National Theatre of the Deaf (NTD), and then for ten years was a leading actor and sign master. Bragg's expertise in the art of Sign Mime for the theatre has received international acclaim. Readers will remember Bragg in *The Quiet Man* TV series as well as in CBS's *A Child's Christmas in Wales* and *And Your Name is Jonah*. He performed on television and Broadway, was an Artist-in-Residence at the Moscow Theatre of Mimicry and Gesture, and taught workshops all over the country. He also served as a goodwill ambassador for the U.S. Department of State during his sabbatical world tour. He co-wrote and directed the play, **Tales from a Clubroom**. His autobiography, **Lessons in Laughter**, was published by Gallaudet University Press in the spring of 1989. In recognition of his extraordinary service to the international world of deaf people in theatre, and in education and communication, he was awarded an honorary doctorate in Humane Letters from Gallaudet University where he has held a unique position as an Artist-in-Residence since 1978 years wear-

**Jack Olson and Bernard Bragg
at Montana State University,
where they first met in 1973**

ing many different hats, such as telling stories in ASL and teaching English idioms through dramatization at Kendall Demonstration Elementary School; giving lectures on deaf culture at Model Secondary School for the Deaf; teaching undergraduate courses: "Comparative Poetics: ASL/English," "The Deaf in Literature," and "Film and Literature;" consulting graduate student teachers on signed communication in the classroom. Currently, he continues to write articles and books and travel extensively here and aboard, conduct workshops on his own creation called Visual Vernacular (a cinematic form of expression) as well as do one-man performances based on his adventures of growing up deaf in America.

Bernard Bragg and Jack Olson met at the National Workshop in Total Communication in the early 1970's where they discovered a mutual interest in the study of sign. Olson, a hearing individual, holds a Bachelor of Arts degree in Communicative Disorders from Pacific University, a Master of Science degree in Special Education of the deaf from Western Oregon College, and a doctorate in Speech and Hearing Science from the Ohio State University. He taught deaf children in Oregon, focusing on speech, drama and football/track. He has been a professor in Communicative Disorders/Speech Communication at Montana State University for more than 25 years and now heads the department. Olson is responsible for creating a number of innovative programs at Montana State University including: the National Workshop in Total Communication, the Summer Language Camp for the Deaf, and the Theatre of Silence, a theatre for both deaf and hearing audiences that has toured extensively in the West, the Midwest, Canada, and most recently China, the Philippines, New Zealand, Australia, Jamaica and numerous European countries. Olson teaches Sign and Sign Mime, and tours with his theatre each spring. He is a certified teacher of the deaf and holds the Certificate of Clinical Competency in Speech Pathology and Audiology. His most recent research project involves the documentation of an emerging deaf culture on the island of Bohol in the Philippines through Project "IDEA" (Olson, 1989, 1992), and the compiling of a series of biographical stories based on his travels, into a reader for deaf high school students entitled **Deaf Communities of the World** (Bridge Publishing, 1994).

PREFACE

Human communication involves rich, highly complex processes. In its highest form, human language, we have the ability to express and understand an incredible range of emotions and information. The user of a language can convey love and hate, despair and ecstacy, certainty and uncertainty. We are enculturated through language, the means through which we perform the mundane activities of everyday life as well as being the vehicle through which we have realized the highest levels of human achievement in literature, philosophy, science and mathematics. Language enables us to move beyond the here and now and to transmit knowledge and learning.

Although most languages are spoken, the nature of human beings is such that, in the case of deaf people, completely developed, sophisticated manual or signed languages have existed since ancient times. Human language may involve print, speech, or signs. Although the channels of communication may put some constraints on the nature of the process, it is vital to remember that all forms have much in common.

One defining characteristic of language, regardless of its form, is the fact that it always involves compromise between the sender and receiver, regardless of whether we are dealing with points, signs, or speech. Any individual sending a message must take into consideration the receiver's knowledge of a particular subject and the receiver's fluency in the language and medium being used. Since the role of sender and receiver may change frequently in person-to-person communication, initial conversations may involve unconscious compromises and negotiations as people establish a common ground for communication.

Effective communicators must show sensitivity, patience, and understanding, or the process will fail. Even if a person has native fluency in a language, there is a need for understanding the position of the other. For example, if a physicist were to try to explain his research to us, he would have to take into consideration both our lack of technical vocabulary in his field and our inexperience. At the same time it is our responsibility to let him know the extent of our knowledge, so that he does not make it too simple.

Nowhere is the need for sensitivity, compromise, and negotiation more evident than in the case of signed communication and sign languages. Although all types of human language have diversity and dialects, signed languages may be unique in that, until recently, prejudice against their use has resulted in fairly large differences in vocabulary and grammar. The lack of print forms of sign languages may also be a factor. For example, in contrasting spoken English and American Sign Language, there is some evidence that the rate of change in spoken English has been slowed by the development and spread of written English. Although new vocabulary is constantly developing, there has been relatively little change in basic grammatical and vocal characteristics. ASL does not have a written form to act as a conservative brake on change. The lack of a written form, in addition to past hostility against its use, may make ASL more susceptible to change and variation than spoken English.

Another factor relates to hearing status. It is logical to assume that a deaf person, relying more heavily on vision, would develop sign fluency in a somewhat different manner than a hearing person, who has probably already developed a spoken language. These are differences, but they are not insurmountable barriers. People of good will have always found effective ways to communicate with each other.

In **Meeting Halfway** two highly skilled individuals share with us the benefits of their experiences, insights, and good will and provide practical information, demonstrations and suggestions for establishment of an effective, non-judgmental environment that is essential for effective communication.

There is evidence of a large and growing number of terms related to sign languages, sign systems and various types of manual communication. We do not wish to add more words to an already redundant vocabulary and have tried to resist the temptation to generate new phrases. We refer in a basic sense to the concept of visual and spatial components of ASL in order to emphasize the three-dimensional nature of sign communication. Reading and writing are also visual, but they are limited to a page, a terminal, or another flat surface. By definition, graphic communication is only two dimensional. Sign occurs in three dimensions length, width, **and** depth, and allows us to utilize an extra dimension to increase the potential richness of our communication.

In this book terms such as "Englished ASL" are used to refer to the type of communication that may occur between individuals in a variety of situations. The goal of this book is to encourage **communication**, even among individuals who do not completely share a full language. ASL, and other sign languages, is extremely complex and has a rich vocabulary and grammar. English, and other spoken languages, is also complex, with a rich vocabulary and grammar. It is not the purpose of this book to help the reader master a complete language, but rather to present a practical guide for the establishment of effective communication.

—Donald F. Moores

INTRODUCTION

Meeting Halfway in American Sign Language is a model text for sign communicators. The communication as signed in the sequential pictures in this book may be seen as *the happy medium* between "pure ASL" and the various Manually Coded English (MCE) systems mainly, because it eliminates more of the unwieldy signed affixes and awkward coinages found in MCE that often block the easy, smooth flow of communication. At the same time, it adds needed ASL principles or "colorings." This book presents a way of bridging the two worlds of people who are deaf and of people who are hearing as communication needs arise.

The strength of the model language as proposed in the sequential pictures in this book and in the following exercises, lies in its eclecticism; the method borrows and incorporates whatever is **needed** from both systems to successfully complete the communicative act effectively. We know that any language is formed and renewed by constant exposure to basic modeling through the natural process of everyday human communication interchange. As Harvey Corson, Senior Vice Presdient of Gallaudet University, has noted (1991): "We need to recognize the fact that we live in one world together; that the deaf community is one segment of a larger society! We need to recognize that it is important to develop one's identity and self-esteem and to learn one's cultural heritage. These are necessary foundations enabling deaf people to bridge our own world to the larger world, which is comprised of people with diverse backgrounds and cultures."

American Sign Language and Generic ASL

In referring to American Sign Language (ASL), often confusion arises as to what the term really means. This is understandable as many people did not realize that it was a viable language until recently. Of course, deaf people **always** knew it was a language! Even among people who sign fluently, however, there have been differences of opinion over the nature of ASL and its relation to English. Is ASL completely different from English or does it contain a number of English features? Does ASL exist on a continuum; that is, do we have different kinds of ASL which in some cases are like English and in other cases are completely different? Are Black and White ASL dialects of the same language, or are they different sign languages? When deaf and hearing people communicate with signs, do they use ASL or some manual code of English or a kind of *pidgin* sign English? Some linguists now talk of *contact* communication between speakers of different spoken languages, and there is an interest in the study of *contact signing* between deaf and hearing individuals and even among deaf individuals themselves. This is the type of communication we are dealing with when we talk of deaf and hearing people meeting halfway in this book.

As the reader might guess, questions of the nature of ASL have been around for a long time. Moores and Stedt (1990) found that discussions and arguments started in 1817, shortly after the establishment of America's first school for the deaf in America in Hartford, Connecticut. The first teacher at that school was Laurent Clerc, a deaf man who had been recruited from a school for the deaf in Paris. Clerc brought with him the French instructional system of "Methodical" signs that had been developed to represent written French. Clerc, with a gift for learning languages, mastered English in a very short time and then modified the French sign system to reflect English. For example, he used the French way of signing days of the week but changed the handshapes to show **M** for Monday, **T** for Tuesday, **W** for Wednesday, **H** for Thursday, etc. He followed similar procedures for naming some colors and for indicating gender.

It has been speculated that Clerc's system interacted with existing sign languages and eventually evolved into what we refer to as ASL. Within a few years of the establishment of the Hartford School, educators were writing about two kinds of signs—"Methodical" signs and "Natural" signs. Methodical signs were closely connected to English and were mostly used in the classroom. Natural signs had a grammar and word order different from English and were mostly used, at first, outside of classes in everyday communication. Although Methodical and Natural sign systems had large shared vocabularies, e.g. signs for weekdays, color, and gender, there were also significant differences. In a short period of time, some schools began to use Natural signs for instruction, with the idea that English could be taught as a second language. A conflict arose in the field of education of the deaf in the United States. Similar debates occurred in other countries with other spoken and sign languages, including France, Germany, Sweden, and Denmark. A sometimes bitter conflict went on for over 50 years among supporters of the two approaches. Unfortunately, both sides lost in 1880 at the International Congress on Education of the Deaf in Milan, Italy, where it was declared that signs of any kind were harmful for deaf children and all instruction should be through oral communication. Although deaf adults continued to use signs in their lives, the use of signs declined in schools, not to reappear in force until the 1970s.

In the 1970's, when signs were reintroduced to classes for deaf children in America, they followed the "Methodical" sign tradition. In other words, they were designed to show English on the hands, and are referred to as Manually Coded English. They include several invented systems the reader may have encountered under such names as Seeing Essential English, Signing Exact English, Signed English, Linguistics of Visual English and Morphemical Sign System. They share a large part of ASL vocabulary, sometimes modified to show initials for English

words. They differ from ASL in that they follow English word order and try to show English grammar in verb tenses, plurals, pronouns, etc. Many educators and linguists argue that the invented manual codes of English are not really languages in themselves, but rather SYSTEMS that represent the English language. On the other hand, ASL is a complete language in its own right.

We are still left with the question of what ASL really is. Everyone would agree that it includes types of signing used by many deaf people and some hearing people, signs that are independent of English, but the question is, does it also include types of signing by both deaf and hearing people that are clearly similar to English? What does ASL include and what does it exclude? Is it inclusive or is it exclusive?

By formal linguistic definition, one might argue that ASL is a language that only includes the traditional concept of American Sign Language and deliberately excludes elements and systems with a strong English flavor. In practice, however, this is often not an easy or practical thing to do. The Gallaudet University faculty, for example, had a series of discussions over developing a working definition of ASL, with some members arguing for a formal, exclusionary definition and others arguing that it should include all of the signing varieties used on campus. One of the authors of this book, Bernard Bragg, pointed out that Webster's Dictionary defines English as the language of the people of England and the U.S. and most of the British colonies. This obviously is a very inclusive definition and it was suggested that the definition of ASL be equally inclusive. The Gallaudet faculty accepted a definition of ASL that included not only the traditional conception of ASL as an independent language, but also types of signing along a continuum approaching English. In expanding on his concept of ASL as an inclusive or generic term, Bragg (1990) stated that we might think of four types of ASL:

1. Traditional ASL

2. Modern ASL

3. Englished ASL

4. Rarefied ASL

At this point we want to present, in detail, our thinking about ASL as a generic term, and to present Bragg's 1990 paper in a somewhat modified form. We want to thank our colleague, Merv Garretson, the editor of the Deaf American monograph, "Communication Issues Among Deaf People" and the National Association of the Deaf for permission to present this material in modified form.

We propose an alternative, more generic definition for American Sign Language. For some time we have felt that the definitions developed within linguistics are too narrow and confining and believe that these linguistic definitions describe only one type of language used within a diverse and dynamic community that contains many varieties and levels of use. We propose a more inclusive and generic perspective on what ASL is and how it is used by deaf people and among deaf and hearing people. This more generic definition of ASL includes all of the varieties of language that American deaf people employ when they sign. Some of the varieties of ASL are heavily influenced by English, the majority language of the United States. Other varieties, especially the variety we call "Traditional ASL," are hardly influenced by English. We believe that the linguistic study of ASL has focused too narrowly on this traditional variety of sign language and not on the full spectrum of American Deaf signing. Our perspective may allow for a deeper and clearer understanding of ASL acquisition on the part of hearing parents and teachers, as well as English acquisition on the part of deaf children.

Before we go any further in our effort to understand the intricacies of language acquisition by hearing people and deaf children and to explore possibilities of eliminating roadblocks to both ASL and English acquisition, we must initially realize that ASL as a generic term is a different way of looking at an old phenomenon. Because there are nearly as many variants to ASL as there are to English, the ASL variants are in the form of at least four major distinct usages.

A quick glimpse at how various individuals communicate among themselves at a given time can give us an idea of which one of the categories each individual uses (some studies describe *contact signing* and *code switching*). Evidently ASL is all-inclusive and adaptable, in relation to both the person one comes in contact with and the subject one wishes to communicate. Surely there is a lot more to ASL than meets the eye, and deaf people are a flexible and creative group of individuals who are adept at doing whatever is necessary to communicate effectively visually and spatially.

(Table 1 presents some of the characteristics of Traditional ASL, Modern ASL, Englished ASL, and Rarified ASL)

Table 1

ASL—A Generic Application

Traditional ASL	Modern ASL	Englished ASL	Rarefied ASL
Holds on to its fixed boundaries	Sustains vague boundaries	Departs from the MCEs in that emphasis is placed on a visually based vocabulary rather than a sound based vocabulary	Takes liberty with the language in poetics and theatre
Is independent of English borrowing or influences	Is heretofore called *Pidgin Sign English* or *Ameslish*		Utilizes *poetic license* in modifying, extending, creating, inventing signs for pictorial effects or emotional qualities
Comprises its own syntactic and semantic features	Comprises a flexible composite of both ASL (traditional) and English	Aims for English accuracy and clarity	
Relies considerably on non-manuals	Incorporates both ASL features and English idioms, phrases	Departs from the MCEs in that it does not incorporate unwieldy signed affixes/tenses	• ASL Poetry
			• Poetry Translation
Maintains fingerspelling to a minimum	Adopts signs that map more directly onto English words	Allows for wordplay as well as creative expression	• Dialogue (Plays)
Allows for continually inventive classifiers	Expands sign vocabulary and relies moderately on fingerspelling	Relies considerably on fingerspelling	• Aesthetics
Employs four dimensional time-space	Allows for easy, smooth flow of communication	Is more readily understood and used when deaf and hearing individuals communicate with each other "cross culturally"	• Visual Vernacular (a cinema form of expression) See page 27.
Allows for sign play as well as creative expression in poetry	Can be called the *middle of the road* or the *happy medium* between Traditional and Englished ASL		

Source: From Bragg, B. 1990. "Communication & The Deaf Community." In M. Garretson (Ed.). **Communication Issues Among Deaf People**. Silver Spring, M.D.: National Association of the Deaf, p. 9.

The strength of ASL lies in its eclecticism in that it borrows and incorporates whatever is needed from various usages to complete the communicative act successfully when deaf people of different backgrounds or when deaf and hearing people communicate. We know that any language is formed and renewed by constant exposure to basic modeling through the natural process of everyday human communicative interchange. Again, the potential for greater communication with ASL lies in its openness to adaptability and creativity; it allows for versatility in artistic and aesthetic signing, thanks to the spatially cinematic nature of the visual medium.

The key to successful language learning and self esteem for deaf children depends in large measure on parental acceptance of deafness and the efficiency of communication interchange between deaf children and their parents. It has been observed that deaf parents exhibit greater parental acceptance of deafness in their children and foster early language acquisition by the early use of gestural/manual communication with their children. (Corson, 1973)

The greater the skill deaf parents demonstrate in various ASL usages, the greater ease deaf children experience language acqusition. This has been noted also in children whose hearing parents learned to sign and signed fluently in their children's formative years.

Unfortunately, there are roadblocks to such acquisition for both hearing parents and teachers. The apprehension of having to learn an entirely different, alien language may hold parents back. Also, the urgency of learning a comprehensible mode of communication that can be used immediately with their deaf child is an awesome challenge.

In view of such challenges, the best possible course for hearing parents to take involves two steps: 1) early survival vocabulary, and 2) formal study. First the parents would learn simple, natural gestures and individual signs without having to learn all of ASL's complex rules and structure. Gilbert Eastman's book **From Mime to Sign** (1989) is an excellent starting point in ASL acquisition, especially for parents who have deaf infants. Next, as infants enter childhood years, the parents would begin to expand their sign vocabulary, as needed, through formal ASL classes and interaction with the deaf community. They would learn more signs while telling their deaf children numerous stories from illustrated story books. Most important of all, hearing parents' willingness and effort to improve their communicative skills in a flexible type of ASL would not only strengthen their relationships with their children but also enhance their children's language learning and self-concept.

With plentiful two-way communication in Traditional/Modern ASL at home with their parents, deaf children would certainly be better equipped when they enter grade school where they would begin sampling Englished ASL. This goes hand-in-hand with the cognitive, affective and motor domains that have a bearing on their language learning. Children can see English in print and on someone else's hands (and lips) as well as *feel* it on their own hands.

Code-switching between ASL and English will be more meaningful to deaf children if it is integrated with real life situations. The often sterile confines of the classroom encourage learning English in superficial ways, thus distancing deaf children from personal involvement with the language so critical to natural development.

Research on the impact of generic ASL on the cognitive development of deaf children is limited at the present time. Anecdotal studies suggest that when we broaden the language environment, we broaden the child's world, for, in Robert Browning's words:

> *"Man's reach must exceed his grasp,*
> *or what's a heaven for?"*

In his original paper, Bernard Bragg made the follow proposal (1990, p.12):

1. Because ASL is a live, dynamic language, changing, evolving, adapting...

2. Because ASL is a visual, spatial, verbal mode—in the hands of individuals, ASL is diverse in style and personality, and, more importantly, may be appreciated for its own distinctiveness...

3. Because ASL stems from deaf people themselves and is part of their psyche—their natural culture, and also because it is a model language to which deaf children may be exposed early in their lives...

4. Because ASL coexists with English in this country—it is open to borrowings, mutations, and other influences; it can be cinematic, poetic, dramatic, or however one wishes to modulate the language...

5. Because ASL is eclectic, versatile, and flexible; it is growing and expanding. Again, because it is adaptable, depending on the person one comes in contact with and also on the subject one wishes to communicate...

6. Because ASL *incidentally or freely* incorporates commonly used English idioms, word order, phrases, colloquialisms and expressions, as well as a number of foreign signs, fingerspelling and initialization...

7. Because ASL utilizes the features of gaze, gesture, facial expression, body position, and lip movements (with or without vocalization) for intelligible, facial communication, and ASL includes its own unique syntactic and semantic features...

8. Because ASL is and should be free from control by any dominant group and also because it may serve as the umbrella of all variation of the language...

THEREFORE, it is proposed that ASL be accepted as the generic term for the linguistic variations which are part of the daily signed communication with the general community who uses it.

The significant sociological and psychological interpretation of American Sign Language (ASL) as an umbrella term for all variations of the language can provide everyone with a feeling of oneness, a sense of belonging for all who communicate visually-spatially. Once accepted as the generic term for linguistic variations, ASL may be used as a catalyst in helping eliminate the awkward, uncomfortable, and uncertain sense of being separated from the mainstream of the deaf community. No longer would the diversity of the language be categorized, departmentalized, discriminated against, nor would signers be compared against each other, judged as superior or inferior.

Once regarded as the generic term, ASL may then be placed in the same vein as spoken English which embraces all dialects, foreign words, slang, or coinages. Peer pressure may be lifted once ASL users feel they are fitting in the mainstream of life within, as well as outside of, the deaf community. After all, communication is the name of the game. It is only through communication that differences in the language would be diminished—certainly *not* through control by any dominant purist/extremist group, such as linguists who wish to decide what language deaf people should communicate in or which language to change. In fact, it is not the language that should be criticized, but rather the person behind the language who should be helped to improve his/her communicative skills.

People should be allowed to express themselves any way they know how or in any language with which they feel comfortable. It is only through the natural process of everyday communicative interchange that the language may flourish.

Our central point is that no language in the world can be controlled. Rather, it is determined by how people use it on a daily basis. William C. Stokoe responded to Bragg with the following poem by Belloc along with the comment which perhaps best sums up this rationale:

> He drew a circle that shut me out:
> Heretic, Rebel, a thing to flout.
> But Love and I had the wit to win;
> We drew a circle that took him in.

ASL draws a large circle: PSE, SEE I, SEE II, Signed English, Ameslan, Ameslish, SSS—all these are names for something that doesn't answer to a name; but they are signing and English is speaking, so why not take them in? I understand your eight reasons as support for the idea that what is signed in America is ASL. (English is spoken, and fingerspelling is a code for *written* English.) It bothers me not at all that you are willing to see ASL as a language with almost as great a variety in its many variants as English itself tolerates.

Discussion on this issue is not solely the preserve of scientists and linguists. Many discoveries and evidence of human progress have occurred outside the laboratory and the test tube. Communication is *not* a rigid science verifiable by only scientific methods; rather, communication is a gentle art. No matter how hard one may try to isolate ASL as different, traditional, insular, free of the influence of other languages—the truth of the matter is that ASL, like any other natural language, will always remain dynamic, flexible, and expandable. ASL can be used in a variety of natural communication settings where individuals with varying ability in ASL negotiate conversation. This phenomenon, referred to by linguists as contact language, is apparent when, for example, intermediate signers enter the deaf community for the first time and attempt to use their newly acquired skills. (Lucas, 1990)

Systems of Communication

The 1960's and 1970's may be viewed as decades of discovery and change in education of the deaf, and the 1980's and 1990's as a time of consolidation. A person enrolled in a training program for education of the deaf some 30 years ago most likely was not given any formal opportunity to learn a sign language. This situation prevails today. However, the Council on Education of the Deaf currently is engaged in revising the national standards for teacher preparation to include both signed and spoken forms of communication. In the past the young educator might learn signed language informally but could not use it in the classroom, at least with younger children. Deaf children were also not given any instruction in signed language by adults, hearing or deaf, although the children would quickly pick up sign language on the playground and in the dormitory. While the native English (hearing) teacher might struggle to use a limited sign vocabulary to create some semblance of *English on the hands*, the typical deaf child would whip through communication with signs accompanied by much body movement and animated facial expressions. This *social* or *natural* sign language of deaf children would not gain much acceptance until years later when sign language was finally studied by linguists who discovered its real worth (Stokoe, 1958). The teachers and parents continued their struggle with manual communication; those who never became very proficient abstained from its use in the end. According to many hearing educators, it was *better* and certainly *easier* to force a deaf child to speak and to speechread because, how else would the deaf child get along in a predominantly *hearing* world?

Then, in the early 1970's, several new pedagogical systems of signing were proposed by educators interested in helping deaf children master the English language. The two most widely studied manually coded English *systems*, each developed by a deaf person, were **Seeing Essential English** (SEE 1), proposed by David Anthony (1971), and **Signing Exact English** (SEE 2), proposed by Gustason, Ptetzinger, and Zwalkow (1972). The phrase **Manually Coded English** is used generically to refer to all artificially developed codes that aim to represent the English language on the hands.

SEE 1 and SEE 2 were developed for parents and teachers of young deaf children as a new tool for communication and education. These sign systems offered a "total communication" package as part of a variety of communication methods (sign, speech, speechreading and writing). Speech could now be simultaneously created in a manual mode, sometimes in an unwieldy manner. Both SEE systems borrowed extensively from ASL. However, according to Van Cleve (1987):

> "When these signs were `borrowed' from ASL, they were altered in dramatic ways. In many cases, one or more significant parts of the sign were changed. The hand shape of many manual alphabets correspond to the initial letter of a particular English word. For example, the flat open handshape that occurs in the ASL sign meaning "happy" or "glad" was replaced with a "g" handshape to represent the English word "glad." This change in handshape creates a new sign, just like replacement of the "c" in "cat" with a "d" creates a new word, "dat." Similarly, the movement of signs in MCE are significantly altered from their appearance in ASL."

SEE 1 and SEE 2 subscribed to the idea that signs should be based on phonetic symbols rather than visual symbols. Therefore, the word "light," even though having a number of different meanings, would be represented by only one sign, because in English there was only one spoken word. Here are some examples of how the word "light" appears in context:

1.   **light** punishment
2.   **light** the fire
3.   it is **light** in here
4.   put on a **light** coat
5.   the load is **light**
6.   do you have a **light**
7.   to shed **light** on
8.   to make **light** of

The context in which the word *light* appears makes the meaning clear, and the educators who developed these sign systems believed that the use of one sign for all these meanings was more compatible with how English was "spoken" by native speakers. However, a hearing child struggling to sort out all of the different meanings in their various contexts has a number of aids available such as pitch, loudness, stress, rising and falling intonation, including years of comprehensible exposure to the linguistic system by which these features can be interpreted. What is natural to the hearing child may not be natural to the deaf child. Because the deaf child is visually oriented, to see *light* meaning electric light, signed as *light* meaning a light load, may be both visually disorienting and incongruous. Some signs have iconic features. For example, "light the fire" depends on the iconic features of striking a match. Signs that are iconic for adults may or may not be iconic for children. Informal observation leads us to believe that it is a characteristic of natural sign languages to use separate signs for visually distinct objects, characteristics or concepts, although again this is a matter that should provide some enlightening research for sign language linguists. Our approach, like other natural sign languages, uses a different sign for each meaning of the word "light" that can be visually discriminated.

Another system, Cued Speech (Cornett, 1967, 1969), uses different hand positions to cue for speechreading. The cues do not convey meaning by themselves and must be used in conjunction with information on the lips in order to be recognized. The American Rochester Method is a combination of the oral method plus fingerspelling. No signs are used and reading and writing are greatly emphasized (Scouten, 1942). Teachers fingerspell every letter of every word synchronized with speech (Quigley, 1969). Neither of these systems has enjoyed the widespread use of the SEE systems.

Meeting Halfway minimizes communication difficulties that may occur in MCE. Signs invented according to rigid rules of English are avoided unless they are accepted by a large number of deaf communicators. Lipsynching, which we use to mean moving the lips but not necessarily voicing is encouraged. Fingerspelling is strongly advocated for words which have no formally accepted signs. We believe our approach is both efficient and effective. It facilitates communication between deaf and hearing people in the clearest and quickest way possible.

Creative Signing

This book provides an opportunity for creative signing in the poetry section. The poems, "Stopping by Woods on a Snowy Evening" by Robert Frost and "Death" by Bernard Bragg, are included for illustration. We use the term "Sign Mime" for this kind of artistic or theatrical signing. It gives the student an opportunity to use "sign play" and freedom of expression. Signed poetry in the aesthetic sense is like no other form of interpretation of literature, since it offers poetic license to take the imagery that someone else has formed in written words, and transform it into a medium which captures the eye. Creative signing is an important part of our approach, emphasizing the flexibility of using the body, face, and surrounding space for better communication. We have termed this aspect "Rarefied ASL."

When translated into Sign Mime, the natural "vocal" rhythm of the words is transformed into a different rhythm in the signing. This should not be a problem. Signs are eloquent in themselves, and they have their own rhythm, often more true to the original concept of the poem than any vocalizing of the words can be. We do not stick to conventional signs only—these are used, sometimes enlarged, or modified or adapted, but often a new sign is created in order to capture the exact meaning of the word in motion. It is an art inspired by words, yet beyond words, and the inner life of the word, the concept behind it, is expressed through hands and face and sometimes the whole body. The rhythm and phrasing, flow and intonation, stress, emphasis, and degrees of volumes, even resonance and tone color can be suggested by the way the movements are made and by variations of pace building to a climax. Mime has great power to encompass and convey meaning, going much deeper than words, but there are realms of intellectual expression which it cannot reach because of its complete disassociation from language. Sign Mime combines the best of both worlds, and in so doing, seems to give a new dimension to the language we take so much for granted. It is not strictly grammatical, but then neither is poetry, and it is in poetic and symbolic drama and in high comedy that the rare quality of the language emerges.

Spoken languages, of course, also have rarefied dialects or elements, the most obvious of which are found in poetry, music, and theatrical productions. The genius and joy of all languages, whether through sign or speech, lie in their almost infinite potential for adaptation to fit an incredible variety of situations.

Visual Vernacular

Performing in Visual Vernacular (the camera eye in action) is a unqiue dimension in Rarefied ASL. Its techniques are cinematic. Visual Vernacular does not involve words or signs. Close-up views, the long shot, the panormaic view, zooming, slow motion, fast motion—all are movements of the human body. The performer remains all the time within the film frame, so to speak, presenting a montage of cross-cuts and cutaway views. Visual Vernacular liberates latent resources of visual self expression in creative signing that leads to a new fluency and dramatic impact.

USING THE MATERIAL

The material in this book is organized in story dialogue form and relates to deaf people and their special world. The sign vocabulary used represents Englished ASL with borrowings from ASL and MCE. Each picture stands for a sign or concept that the student needs to study and imitate and represents a *programmed* approach to the learning of sign. Although the pictures used are *static* and in themselves do not show *movement*, the sequencing of the pictures as one would read a *sentence* demonstrates how the signs flow and relate. Descriptions and comments are given below the pictures to help the student see more readily what is to be learned. For example, there will be a number of additional clues that a student can obtain from reading these descriptions. There will be handshape clues, movement clues, and starting and ending clues that might not be totally comprehensible from viewing the pictures alone. A menu for these clues and other suggestions for use is provided.

Categories of Signing

Our system utilizes a number of ideas from ASL. We have categorized all signs into five groupings from the ASL base to help the reader remember and properly use visual-spatial communication. The five categories are:

(1) **COMBO-SIGN**
(2) **PARA-SIGN**
(3) **PICTO-SIGN**
(4) **DACTO-SIGN**
(5) **INITI-SIGN**

COMBO-SIGN. *Compounding*, a natural process for developing signs in ASL, has been described by Bellugi and Newkirk (1980) and is labeled in this text as COMBO-SIGN. Compounding has been used extensively in SEE I and SEE II, as well as the Gallaudet Signed English System developed by Bornstein (1973) and others. For example, the sign for "precious" can be made by first signing "valuable" followed by an "e" handshape on the chin changing into a fist. Another way to sign this word involves the sign for "good" followed by both hands moving to the heart. A third includes "sweet" followed by "important." We would not use any of these combinations for the concept "precious" metals. The meaning here is very different and would be safer to fingerspell for clarity. Other examples of COMBO-SIGNS are:

income = *money* + *earn*
choir = *sing* + *group*

There are numerous other signs that combine signs to create a concept. For example:

laundry = *wash* + *room*
agree = *think* + *same*
desert = *dry* + *land*
confuse = *think* + *mix*
deaf = *ear* + *closed* , or *ear* + *mouth*
and so on.

PARA-SIGN. Since English is rich in synonyms, the possibilities for replacing a "non-sign" word with a signable synonym are almost limitless. In this book we call the exchanged word a PARA-SIGN. This practice also gives us an opportunity to make better use of our fairly limited supply of signs. Examples in this category are as follows:

offered/presented,
startled/surprised,
sympathy/pity,
trapped/stuck
fortunate/lucky.

So when you want to use the sign "offered" in a sentence, it is all right to use the sign for "present," but make sure that you carefully mouth the word (lipsynch) to differentiate the two words. Sometimes one sign will have several different PARA possibilities such as "present," "offer," "suggest," and "propose." The process of **lipsynching** can best be described as the synchronization of the articulated lip movement (English) with the movement of the hands/fingers for the **same** word. This may be no easy task, dependent upon the skill of the signer/articulator and the lip-reading abilities of the deaf recipient. Usually some speed/fluidity will be necessarily sacrificed. Remember that many teachers who use MCE fail to do this very task in a skillful fashion. They are criticized for leaving out part of the code, usually the sign code. The effort needed to become skillful in both modalities is usually worth it, considering the valuable additional information that is brought to the communication situation.

PICTO-SIGN

PICTO-SIGN. "Mimetic signs" as described by Bellugi and Newkirk (1980) are similar to our category PICTO-SIGN. PICTO-SIGNing involves the creation of signs that are iconic in nature, or easily recognized by an audience as representing real objects or events. For example, it is possible to go through the category of animals, give the sign for each animal before a group of non signers and link the proper animal to its sign. Examples of PICTO-SIGNS in this book include the word "icebreaker" from the story "The Three Whales Who got Stuck in the Ice." Here the sign for "boat" is made and the forward movement of the ship battering away at the ice is indicated by the back and forth movement of the cupped hands. Sometimes a whole phrase can become PICTO-SIGNed, such as "sank out of sight" (this is from the same story and refers to one of the whales who died and sank to the bottom of the ocean). A slow downward twisting movement of the hand is all that is needed to understand this concept in the context of the entire story. Another phrase, "surface of the water" (both hands palms down, flutter fingers while moving the two hands apart). **Lipsynching** becomes **very** important in PICTO-SIGNing, especially whenever a phrase is involved. This is not to suggest that ASL is an iconic language or formalized version of mime. Linguistic research has found that ASL is, indeed, primarily an arbitrary language. (Bellugi and Klime, 1979.)

DACTO-SIGN. This category uses fingerspelling for **emphasis or clarity**. In the sentence, "I will not allow you to go home **if** you don't finish your work first!" the word "if" can be fingerspelled with emphasis (perhaps include an outward movement of the hand) along with appropriate facial expression and voice. That same word could also be signed with emphasis as an option. The important thing to remember here is that by fingerspelling with intensity, the sign can take on **added** meaning just as it would if the communicator were adding intonation or inflection to his/her voice. Fingerspelling for clarity is an easy concept to understand. In the story "The Beefeater Catastrophe," there is no sign for that specialized drink "Beefeater." In SEE II this concept would be broken up by combining the signs "beef" and "eat" plus the "er" ending. For us, fingerspelling "beefeater" and carefully lipsynching it would be the proper procedure. Fingerspelling, along with careful lipsynching, will **not** take the place of clearly communicating different concepts and meanings that might arise from the use of the **same** English word that has more than one meaning. For example, the word "run" has many meanings:

(1)   run to the store

(2)   run in my stocking

(3)   he has the runs (diarrhea)

(4)   run in a marathon

(5)   to run for office

Each of these may need to be signed differently for clear understanding, especially for deaf children. Additionally, there is a whole body of words that the authors consistently spell out when needed: **is**, **to**, **he**, **she**, **him**, **the**, **a**, **an**, **had been**, **have been**, **there**, (if needed), **of**, **out**, **up**, (with verbs like "look out," "look up," "put up,") **was**, **were** (if needed), **as**, and **such**. The invented signs from MCE may not follow ASL principles. One should remember that it requires less effort to simply **spell** them and include that movement in with the sign flow rather than reaching up to some spot on the head ("h**e**," "hi**m**," "sh**e**," "her") or assuming another position that requires more physical movement ("ha**v**e," "ha**s**," "ha**d**,") thus hindering the fluidity. In this text, a lot of pointing with the index finger is done. In the context of the sentence and with proper lipsynching, the pointing is sufficient. The category of DACTO-SIGN includes, but is not limted to, loan signs such as: "car," "job,"and "<u>o</u>pportunity." These words were fingerspelled originally and, over time, have become accepted as independent signs.

INITI-SIGN. This is a way of **initializing** signs (picking up the first letter of a word to be signed) to provide an added clue for the receiver. In ASL, for example, the days of the week are initialized for this purpose, so is **C**hristmas and hundreds of others. **F**urniture and **f**rench **f**ries are both INITI-SIGNS and the only difference is in the manner in which they are produced. In the first the "f" is moved back and forth in small, short arcs, palm out, about chest height. In the second, the same hand configura-tion is used in the same position, but two short jabs of the hand while moving the hand slightly to the right suffices for comprehension. **C**hristmas is produced several different ways, depending upon what part of the country you hail from. Typically, a "c" is moved in a short curved sweep in front of the chest. **C**hocolate is made with the "c" hand configuration of the right hand making small circles (palm out) while touching the top of the fist of the left hand. There are hundreds of initialized signs to be used. We use the initialized signs that deaf people in general have invented or accepted and made their own.

Use of the Body and Face

The reader is also encouraged to use the face and body expressively as well as to give attention to the following principles of signing:

(1)   speed variation

(2)   degree of intensity or force

(3)   size of sign variation

(4)   awareness of the **place** a sign is made and the direction a sign moves

(5)   movement of head and shoulders

(6)   focus of eyes

(7)   eye brow movement

(8)   right/left alternation in order to create a clear imagery

All of these suggestions give extra meaning to the signed message. The face and body are valuable resources. An individual with at least a minimal knowledge of sign should be aware of the importance and communicative potential for using these parameters. For illustration, consider the following humorous story, which is a shorter version of James Thurber's "Little Red Riding Hood."

"My **dear**, I have your basket **already packed**. Promise you won't eat the cookies I baked for grandmother!"

> **dear** (*sugar*)
> **already** (*finish*)
> **packed** (mimed packing cookies in the basket, with focus of eyes downward toward the child, with questioning look in eyes)

"Can't I eat just a few?"

> (reposition body slightly, change eye focus up toward the adult) question in eyes

"Yes, **of course**. Remember **not to** talk **to** any **strangers** on the **road** or **in the woods**."

> (change eye focus downward)
> **of course** (*natural*)
> **not** (palms down cross hands, separate)
> **to** (fingerspell) optional
> **to** (use sign)
> **strangers** (PARA "new" + person sign)
> **road** (PARA "way")
> **in the woods** (fingerspell "in the" allowing the movement to flow into the sign for "woods" fingerspell "the" is optional)

"Oh, Mother, you always **treat** me like I have no sense!"

> **treat** (PARA "control," "handle," "direct")
> reposition body, refocus eyes up

"Goodbye now!"

> reposition body, refocus eyes downward

"Goodbye. I'll call you when I **get there**."

> reposition body, refocus eyes up
> **get there** (PARA "arrive")

(**she** left the house and **walked** through the woods, **picking flowers as she went along**—suddenly a big wolf appeared)

> **she** ("girl" + point)
> **walked** (create the sign for "walk" but use more energy as if "skipping along"—be sure to include appropriate facial expression for "joyful discovery")
> **picking flowers as she went along** (mime include careful lipsynch)

"**Hi**, can I help you?"

> reposition body, refocus eyes
> **Hi** (ASL wave)

"Yes, where is my grandmother's house?"

> reposition body, refocus eyes up

"Follow this road until you arrive at the **dead end**, then go right. There you will find your grandmother's house."

> **dead end** (PARA "against")

"Oh, thank you very much!"

> reposition body, refocus eyes up

(she arrived, and **opened the door)**

> **she** ("girl" + point)
> **opened the door** (mime movement with
> lipsynch)

"Grandmother, what has happened to you?"

(she pulled out the gun from her basket and **pointed it at the** wolf who was dressed like her grandmother with a nightgown and cap)

> **she** ("girl" + point)
> **pulled out the gun from her basket**
> (PICTO-SIGN movement)
> **pointed** (keep the RH configuration for "gun"
> and aim it at the wolf)
> **at** (fingerspell)
> **the** (fingerspell) optional

(a red flag **popped out of the gun** that said "bang"—**another message** on the flag said, "You can't fool little girls **now-a-days like you used to!")**

> **popped out of the gun** (PICTO-SIGN
> hand mime a flag unfolding from
> gun with your left hand)
> **another** (PARA "other")
> **message** (PARA "word")
> **now-a-days** (PARA "today")
> **like** (ASL "y")
> **you used to** (over the shoulder motion "past")

The principles outlined in the preceding story can be emphasized or de-emphasized for demonstration purposes. The ideas for improving communication should be obvious ones—the signer creates a miniature story or play as the communication takes place, and should feel free to expand on the idea of "setting up" people and places within surrounding space and to use classifers as needed to characterize the people and events involved in the story. This story and other stories in **Meeting Halfway** effectively demonstrate these principles.

Additional Suggestions

(1)   We suggest dropping most of the affixes, especially word endings, for fluidity purposes. Prefixes and suffixes, however, can and should be added for **explicit comprehension**—but they should be created subtly (smaller). For example, avoid making the "ing" appear as a separate word. Sign it small and short, and blend it into the root word.

(2)   Unsigned tenses are often made clear by context, as well as by careful lipsynching.

(3)   Fingerspell "it" and emphasize with the opposite hand by pointing to the "it" being fingerspelled. This will help to clarify the importance and meaning of "it." Also such signs as "if," "but," "or," "no," and "yes" can be fingerspelled for emphasis.

(4)   Use spatial relationships to create a clear picture. Once you set up and establish a reference point—be consistent. Avoid changing places. Also, clearly "index" about whom or to whom you are talking.

(5) **Do not sign every word**. By attempting to sign **every** word, the whole signing process will slow down. The key is to find the right balance and include information on the hands **and** on the mouth according to the communicative situation.

(6) If possible, incorporate rarefied ASL. In rarified ASL, the key is creativity and expressiveness. Remember, you want to express yourself artistically and in an open, uninhibited manner. The message is important, not the grammar.

(7) Use of classifiers. One sign technique that is relatively easy to understand and incorporate into the ASL Model Language is the use of ASL "classifiers." These "classifiers" are various hand shapes that represent a noun and show **location** and also possible **action** of that noun. For example, the vertically raised index finger of the fisted hand shape could represent a person who could move from one spot to another, go up or downstairs or in an elevator, or meet another person (when the two identical fisted handshapes with index's raised are brought together). Another one of many possibilities might be to use this "classifier" shape to represent telephone poles zipping by outside a bus or train window. The speed of the train or bus could be represented by the speed of movement of the hand (as the poles go by the window). Still another "classifier" of this type is the "3" handshape that represents a motorized land or water vehicle (car, bus, truck, van, or boat). For example, the sentence "The car stopped and backed into the parking spot"

could all be communicated with the "3" handshape held in a horizontal position. Similarly, a boat could be represented as it moves forward through choppy water.

"Classifiers" that are used to indicate **size**, **shape**, and **texture** of a noun as well as its location in space usually incorporate both hands. Think how you might indicate the following concepts:

(1) a long, curved, narrow pole

(2) a rough tree stump or craggy branch with Spanish moss hanging down

(3) a medium-size telephone pole

(4) a rectangular bridge support (4' x 6')

(5) a square poster

(6) your checkbook

(7) buttons on your shirt

(8) eye glasses

Here are some more commom classifier handshapes for you to practice. Your teacher or native deaf signer might be able to help you discover more!

Think of the handshape that you would need:

1. stripes/plaids (sign is made with one hand, at the shoulder)
   prison bars (two hands)
   movie (two hands, flickering image)

2. write with a pen (mime movement)
    apply lipstick, eyeshadow (mime movement)
    outline a picture frame (mime movement)

3. catch a soft ball (be sure to mime movement, use just
        the one hand)
    turn a door knob (mime movement)
    hold a basket ball (2 hands)

4. camera flash (mime movement)
    water coming out of a shower (mime movement)
    suction (mime movement)
    light on, light off (mime movement)

5. hold on to barebells (mime movement)
    hold on to a stick shift (mime movement)
    hold on to a hammer (mime movement)

6. a pistol
    an innoculation device

7. a tooth brush (mime movement of brushing your teeth)
    several hotdogs on a grill (mime movement)

Practice these handshape with your classmates and consider
incorporating them into your signing repertoire. Signing will be
clearer, more fun, and the additional information imparted is
worth the effort! See page 150-156 for 43 classifier handshape
pictures and additional exercises.

A WAKE-UP CALL FOR HEARING SIGNERS

Bernard Bragg

If you prefer to use voice while signing to me (*because you are used to hearing your own voice while speaking*), please don't leave out too many signs while signing to me. I don't read lips very well, so I depend a lot more on your signing than on your lips.

If you prefer to use voice while signing to me (*because you usually think better through hearing yourself speak*), please be reminded that prepositions, pronouns, or even articles, are sometimes as essential as the verbs or nouns you use visually.

If you prefer to use voice while signing to me (*because it helps you to express yourself more lucidly or feelingly*), please be sure to inflect your signing the way you inflect your voice. After all, you are not speaking to yourself. I am the one who is listening to you, so I depend not only on what you say but also on how you express yourself.

If you prefer to use voice while signing to me (*because you are also thinking of those who are hard-of-hearing*), please remember that it is not easy to communicate clearly if you have to speak and sign at the same time. You need to modulate your speaking so that your signing does not suffer.

If you prefer to use voice while signing to me (*because your spoken language is your native language*), please remember how important it is to maintain eye contact with me so that you can see whether I follow you or not. After all, words to the ear are **not** the same as words to the eye.

If you prefer to use voice while signing to me (*because you may not be fluent in traditional ASL as you are in English*), please make sure that your phrasing, pausing, and pacing are appropriate for the eye. After all, speaking for the ear and signing for the eye are two different modes, so you need to find the right balance in your expression.

If you prefer to use voice while signing to me (*because you are conscious of phonetics*), please remember to try to fingerspell words as clearly as you can, even if it blocks your speech flow. After all, you are and should be more concerned with how you communicate visually than with how you sound to yourself or to other people who can hear you.

Menu

The following "menu" is designed to help the student better deal with the descriptions under the pictures in the story and with the exercise portion of this text. If any sign in this "menu" is **not** familiar, the reader should look up the sign in any standard sign language dictionary or text. A good one is Sternberg, Martin, **American Sign Language: A Compreshensive Dictionary**, New York: Harper Collins Publishers, 1981. It is available in several editions. The examples selected for "key" signs are all very common and should be in a signer's receptive/expressive sign vocabulary. Examples are shown on the next page.

In the following stories and dialogue, you will note the intermittent signs in between photos, as follows:

- •
- • A vertical three-dot indicates the end of a sentence.
- •

- •
- P
  A
  U   indicates the end of a clause or a phrase.
  S
  E
- •

Whenever a sign has more than one meaning, i.e., "native," "natural," "nation," the reader will find an extra smaller head-shot behind the regular picture (see page 111). This shows how word-mouthings ("lipsynch") can help make clear which meaning one wishes to use.

Sign movement	Key signs
arc	*thing* or *children*
tap	*often* or *work*
wiggle	*fingerspell* or *wait*
flutter	*butterfly* or *fish*
sweep	*all day* or *sing*
upward	*feel* or *full (as in eating)*
downward	*depressed* or *relief*
forward	*continue* or *proceed*
outward	*go* or *look forward*
inward	*come* or *mine*
backward	*we (ASL)* or *struggle*
sideways	*plan* or *ready*
vertical	*grew up* or *upward*
alternating	*walk* or *race*
bend	*yes* or *flexible*
twist	*key* or *sour*
strike	*hit* or *destroy*
cross	*across* or *influence*

Sign movement	Key signs
shake	*English* or *pepper*
wave	*movie*
slash	*bread* or *what*
brush	*sugar* or *paint*
rocking	*weigh* or *suffer*
circle around	*situation* or *world*
repeat	(once) *this*
	(twice) *owe*
orientation of palms	*your vs mirror*
	school vs separate
circular	(one hand) *always*
	(two hands) *sin*
	(inward) *come*
	(outward) *go*
	(two hands alternate) *sign*
eye focus	(look up, down, sideways, around, etc.)
fingerspell	(the, he, she, it, to, of, a, if, her, him, etc)

Fingerspelled (fs) words, as shown below, are optional — not required unless needed for clarity or emphasis:

The following boxes are included in Bernard Bragg's story and dialogue:

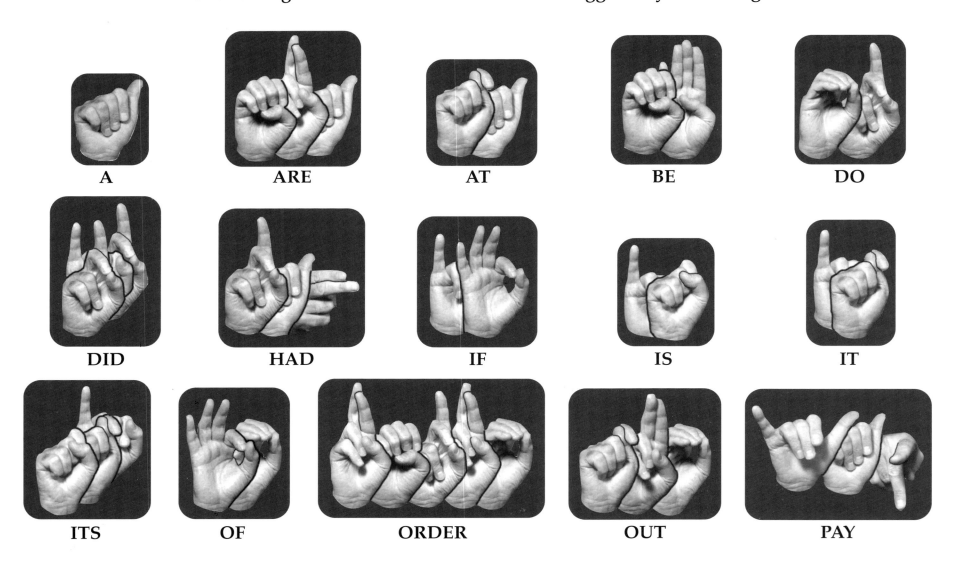

A	ARE	AT	BE	DO
DID	HAD	IF	IS	IT
ITS	OF	ORDER	OUT	PAY

SO   THE   TO   WAS

WELL   WERE

The following boxes are included in Jack Olson's story and dialogue:

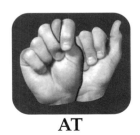
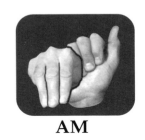
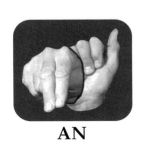
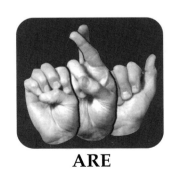

A   AT   AM   AN   ARE

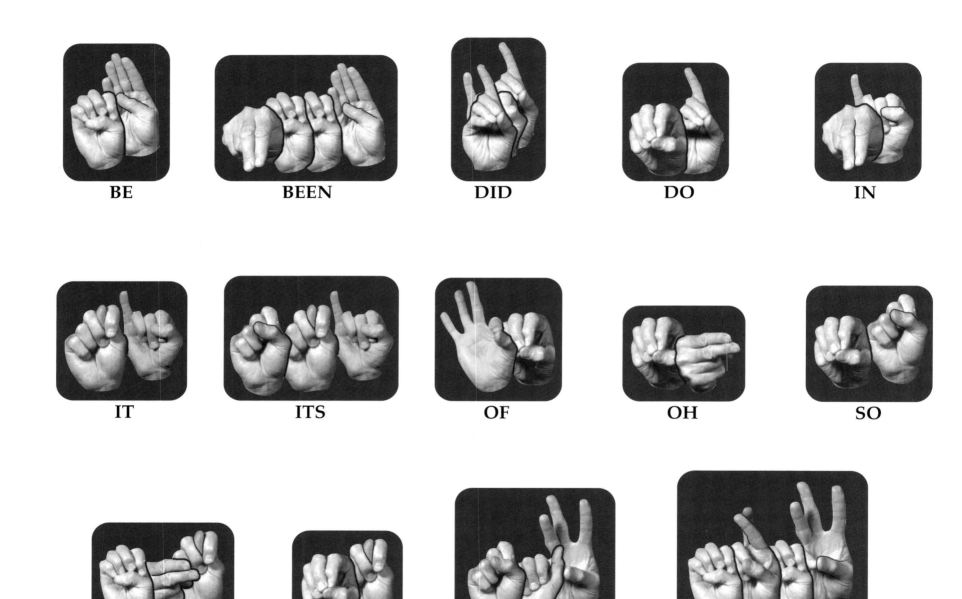

BE BEEN DID DO IN

IT ITS OF OH SO

THE TO WAS WERE

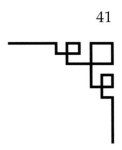

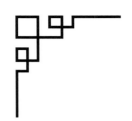

STORIES,

DIALOGUE,

&

POEMS

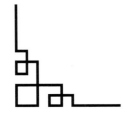

CRACKERS

Some examples of special signs used in the following story "Crackers"

PICTO   grow up (show height)
            smash (strike, twist fists)
            Scottish (plaid)
            choke (grab throat)

PARA   custom = "tradition", "habit"
            chuckle = "laugh"
            omen = "luck"
            superstitious = "imaginative"
            often = "frequent"
            lot = "many"

DATO   if, but, so (fingerspell for emphasis)

INITI   **g**roup, **r**estaurant, **p**erson, **r**ealize, etc.

ASL
SIGNS: can't,
            didn't,
            don't know,
            grew up,
            picked up,
            carry it on,
            watch (follow eye focus),
            had to

CRACKERS

Bernard Bragg

I had often wondered about the sign for "crackers." For the life of me I could not figure out what crackers had to do with the elbow! I asked many different people if they could tell me about this sign, but they did not know. I grew up wondering about it. Then one day I was in London eating in a restaurant with a group of actor friends. We were eating soup and talking at the same time. A movie actor who sat on my left was talking to the others. Since I was the only deaf person at this table I could not pay much attention to the conversation. I was busy eating soup, but something to my side caught my attention. My actor friend picked up a cracker from a bread basket and brought it under his arm and smashed the cracker against his elbow. I almost choked on my soup, but then I immediately realized that this was where we got the sign. I was wondering why he did that, so I asked him to please explain to me why he had to break the crackers with his elbow. He looked at me and chuckled and said, "Well, that is a Scottish custom that I grew up with. The people in Scotland are very superstitious—you know! They believe that if you can break a cracker into three pieces with your elbow it means a good omen." He added that you could almost cheat using both hands to break the cracker, but you can't cheat using the elbow. I said to him, "This is the most exciting discovery I have ever made in my whole life." He asked me to show him the sign for it and I said, "You sign it exactly as you do it!" I added, "This sign must be 150 years old, and both of us are still carrying it on—you with your real crackers and me with my sign!"

I [had]

option: sign "finish"

often

motion: *tap on palm*
para: "frequent"

wondered

motion: *circular,
alternating*

about [the]

motion: *forward,
circular, alternating*

sign

motion: *either outward or
inward, circular, alternating*

for

motion: *outward*

motion: *bend or twist*

"crackers."

motion: *tap on elbow twice*

For [the]

motion: *outward*

life

motion: *upward*

[of] me

● P A U S E ●

I

couldn't

motion: *RH downward
head shake*

figure [out]

motion: *cross hands twice*

what

motion: *RH downward*

crackers

had

motion: *inward*
option: *fingerspell*

 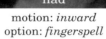

[to do]   with

[the] elbow!

motion: *tap*

I

asked

motion: *downward*

many

motion: *outward*
once or twice

different

motion: to the side,
repeat twice

people

motion: *outward*
circular, alternating

[if]

they

motion: *sweeping (l to r)*
option: *fingerspell*

could

motion: *downward*
Note: *lipsynch*

tell me

motion: *downward*

about

motion: *forward,*
circular, alternating

this

option: *ASL ("Y" downward)*

sign,

motion: *either outward or*
inward, circular, alternating

PAUSE

but

motion: *move apart*
option: *fingerspell*

they

motion: *sweeping (l to r)*
option: *fingerspell*

didn't know.

ASL type
option: *fs "did"*
sign "not know"

I

grew up

motion: *upward*
PICTO: *show height (ASL)*
option: *sign "grew" fingerspell "up"*

wondering

motion: *inward,*
circular, alternating
option: *add "ing"*

about [it.]

motion: *forward,*
circular, alternating

Then

motion: *outward*
option: *fingerspell*

one

day

motion: *downward*

I [was]

in

motion: *downward*

London

motion: *outward, circular*

eating

motion: *repeat twice*
option: *add "ing"*

in

motion: *downward*

[a] restaurant
INITI: *"r"*
motion: *l to r*

with

[a] group [of]
INITI: *"g"*
motion: *outward,
circular, twist*

actor
motion: *inward, circular,
alternating;
then downward*

friends.
motion: *index fingers
alternate*

We

[were]   eating
motion: *repeat twice*
option: *add "ing"*

soup
PICTO: *mime*
motion: *repeat twice*

and
motion: *move from
left to right*

talking
motion: *outward back and
forth, alternating*
option: *add "ing"*

[at the]   same
motion: *index fingers meet*

option: *ASL type ="time" + two-hand "Y" — "Y"*

time.
motion: *single tap*

[A]   movie
PICTO: flickering screen
motion: *right-hand "waving"*

actor
motion: *inward, circular,
alternating;
then downward*

who
motion: *circle
around mouth*

sat

motion: *downward*

on

my

left

Use left hand
Note: ASL eye focus

[was]   talking

motion: *outward back
and forth alternating*
option: *add "ing"*

to

[the]   others.

motion: *l to r*

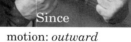

Since

motion: *outward*

I   [was]

[the] only

motion: *twist palm in*

deaf

motion: *from ear to chin*

person

motion: *outward,
cirulcar, alternating*

[at the]   table,

PICTO

I

couldn't

ASL type
motion: *RH downward*

[pay] much

attention

motion: *outward*

to

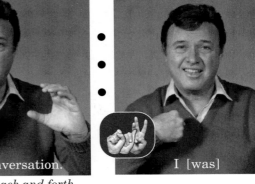

[the] conversation.

motion: *back and forth*
alternating
PARA: *Communication*

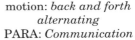

I [was]

busy

INITI: "b"
motion: *back and forth*
sideways

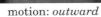

eating

motion: *circular, alternating*
Option: *add "ing"*

soup,

motion: *repeat twice*
Note: *"eating soup" is mimed*

P
A
U
S
E

but

option: *fingerspell*

something

motion: *index finger shaking*
slightly, then arc to right

to

Option: *fingerspell*

my

motion: *cross hands twice*

side

motion: *downward*

caught

motion: *both hands close*
as if to catch a ball

my

attention.

option: *ASL type for "caught my eye" (index finger to eye, then point left)*

My

actor

motion: *circular, alternating, then downward*

friend

motion: *fingers alternate*

picked up

motion: *upward*

[a] cracker

motion: *tap on elbow twice*

from

motion: *RH move away from index finger*

[a]   bread

motion: *repeat twice*
PICTO: *slice the loaf*

basket

PICTO: *shape of basket*

and

motion: *l to r*

brought

motion: *inward*

[it]   under

motion: *RH outward*

his

motion: *to the side*

arm

motion: *RH l to r*

and

motion: *l to r*

smashed

motion: *fist twist and strike on elbow*

[the] cracker

motion: *tap on elbow twice*

against

motion: *tap on palm*

his

motion: *to the side*

elbow.

motion: *tap*

I

almost

motion: *fingers brush knuckles, upward*

choked

mime

on

my

soup,

but

motion: *to the side*

then

motion: *right index from thumb to finger*

I

immediately

option: *fingerspell "ly"*

realized

motion: *circular*
PARA: *"thought"*

that

motion: *tap*

this [was]

where

motion: *back and forth
sideways*

we

motion: *r to l*

got

motion: *inward*

[the] sign

motion: *circular, alternating*

from.

motion: *RH move away
from index*

I [was]

wondering

motion: *circular, alternating*
option: *add "ing"*

why

motion: to the side

he

option: *fingerspell*
Note: *eye focus*

did

motion: *back and forth
sideways*

that,

motion: *tap*

•
P
A
U
S
E
•

so

DACTO

I	asked	him	[to] please	explain
	motion: *downward* ASL: *point index out, flick (as if asking a question)*	option: *fingerspell*	motion: *circular, clockwise*	motion: *outward back and forth alternating*

to	me	why	he	had to
option: *fingerspell*		motion: *downward*	option: *fingerspell*	motion: *downward* option: *fingerspell*

break	[the] crackers	with	his	elbow.
motion: *two fists separate* PICTO	motion: *tap on elbow*		motion: *to the side* ASL: *eye focus*	

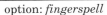

He

option: fingerspell

looked

ASL type: directional

[at]   me

and

chuckled

motion: repeat twice
PARA: "laughed"
note: "lipsynch"

and

motion: bend or twist

said,

motion: small outward,
circle off chin, repeat twice

" "

["Well,]   that   [is]

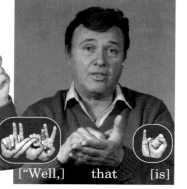

[a]   Scottish

motion: RH turn over
PICTO: plaid

custom

PARA: "tradition"
or "habit"

that

I

grew up

PICTO: show height (ASL)
option: sign "grow"
fingerspell "up"

with.

55

motion: outward, circular, alternating

[The] people

in

Scotland

PICTO: *plaid*

[are]   very

motion: to the side

superstitious

motion: *outward, circular, alternating*
PARA: "imagine"
Note: move eyes upward, back and forth

you

know!

motion: *tap on forehead*

They

believe

motion: *RH tap on palm*

that

motion: *tap*

if

DACTO
option: *ASL "i" on cheekbone*
Note: *fs for emphasis*

you

can

motion: *downward*

break

motion: *two fists separate*
PICTO

[a]   cracker

motion: *tap on elbow twice*

into

motion: *RH r to l*

three

pieces

motion: *slice*

with

your

motion: *outward*

elbow,

motion: *tap*

P A U S E

[it]   means

motion: *twist*

[a]   good

motion: *outward*

omen."

PARA: *luck*
Note: *fingerspelled because
there is no sign*

He

option: *fingerspell*

added

motion: *RH touch LH*

that

you

could

motion: *downward*

almost

motion: *RH brush knuckles*
Note: *ASL facial expression*

cheat

Note: *ASL facial expression*
Note: *many other local signs*

using

INITI: "u"
motion: *right hand circular,
repeat twice*

both

motion: *RH downward*
PICTO

hands

motion: *slice*

to

option: *fingerspell*

break

PICTO
motion: *two fists separate*

[the] cracker,

motion: *tap on elbow twice*

● **P A U S E** ●

but

you

can't

motion: *fingertips strike
downward*

cheat

motion: *r to l*

using

INITI: "i"
motion: *circular*
option: *add "ing"*

[the] elbow.

motion: *tap on elbow*

● ● ●

I

said

motion: *circular, outward*

to

him
option: *fingerspell*

" "

"This [is]

[the]   most
motion: *RH upward*

exciting
motion: *outward, circular,
alternating*
option: *add "ing"*

discovery
Note: *ASL enlarged sign;
upward*

I

have
option: *fingerspell*
ASL *"finish"*

ever
motion: *outward*
option: *fingerspell*

made
motion: *twist*

in

my

whole
motion: *half circular*
PARA: *"all", "entire"*

life."
INITI: *"l"*
motion: *upward*

He

option: *fingerspell*

asked

motion: *downward*

me

[to] show

motion: *outward*

him

option: *fingerspell*

[the] sign

motion: *circular, alternating*

for [it]

motion: *outward*

and

motion: *l to r*

I

said

motion: *outward, small
circular, off chin,
repeat twice*

" "

"You

Note: *eye focus throughout
the quote*

sign

motion: *inward, circular,
alternating*

exactly

motion: *half circular,
alternating, tap once*
Option: *fingerspell "ly"*

[as] you

do

motion: *back and forth sideways*
option: *fingerspell*

it!"

DACTO

I

added,

motion: *RH tap on LR*

" "

"This

sign

motion: *inward, circular, alternating*

must

motion: *downward*

be

DACTO

150

motion: *"1"—"C"—"50"*

years

motion: *circular*

old

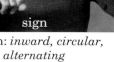

and

motion: *l to r*

both

motion: *RH downward*

of

DACTO
option: *fingerspell*

us
ASL type
motion: *back and forth*

are
DACTO
option: *ASL sign "true"*

still
motion: *outward*

carrying
motion: *two arcs downward*
option: *add "ing"*

[it]   on —
motion: *outward*
PARA: *"continue" or "last"*

· P A U S E ·

you
motion: *follow eye focus*

with

your
motion: *outward*
follow eye focus

real
PARA: *"true"*

crackers
motion: *tap on elbow*

and
motion: *l to r*

me

with

my

sign!"
motion: *circular, alternating*

EXPERIENCES OF A HEARING EDUCATOR

Some examples of special signs used in the following story

PICTO   exposed (LH raised index, represents a person, RH
             hand shape "o" then opens to "5" and palm tap LH
             index)
             community (tops of roofs)
             camp (tents)

PARA   unusual = "different"
             fluidity = "smoothness"
             drawn = "attracted" or "fascinated"
             means = "method," "way," or "approach"
             apparent = "obvious" or "clear"

DACTO   if, in, but, etc.

COMBO   playground

INITI   method, Oregon, system, communication, oral, pure,
             adults, dorms, math, university, graduate, training,
             program, language, attitude, qualities, individuals,
             person, cultures, world, developed, conceptually

ASL
SIGNS: fluent
             exposed
             sort of
             drawn

"Experiences of a Hearing Educator"

Jack Olson

I was 23 years old when I first became interested in the oral and manual communication of deaf people. I was studying to become a teacher of the deaf at the Oregon School. The first system of signing I learned was pure SEE. I became fluent in this method and felt proud to be able to communicate with deaf children and deaf adults so quickly!

However, it soon became apparent to me that there was another system being used by the children on the playground and in the dorms. I watched this system being used from a distance--sometimes understanding some, but mostly understanding nothing. It was really very confusing to me. This other system called ASL did not follow English word order. The other teachers told me that we didn't need to learn ASL. It would not help deaf children learn their English better!

I taught deaf children for 2 years. I taught speech, reading, and math and also was the football and track coach. All the time I used the pure MCE technique with my students. Later, after 2 more years of graduate school, I started teaching at the university level and established a training program for teachers of the deaf.

I became exposed to more and more ASL through my travels with a theater for deaf children and a summer language camp. My attitude toward this unusual language began to change and I began to accept it for its fluidity and theatrical qualities. I thought to myself, "What a fool I was for ignoring what ASL had to offer—both for the deaf community and also for those hearing individuals who are interested in working with them."

There I stood, sort of like a person in between two cultures—the older I became and the more experiences I had with the deaf world, the more I was drawn to the idea of learning ASL. Then I met Bernard Bragg. We became good friends and, over many years, we developed our own means of communicating with each other that combines ASL and English. We call this approach **Englished ASL**, and we are very excited about using it with anyone who communicates in this language.

Each day I think that I am becoming more and more pleased with my signing, and now I really feel good about my changed attitude.

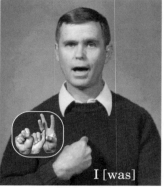

I [was]

option: *"I" handshape on chest (formal)*

twenty-three

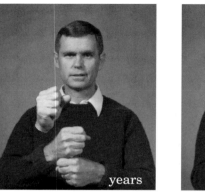

years

motion: *circular, outward*

old

motion: *downward*

when

motion: *circular, then touch*

I

first

motion: *touch*

became

motion: *rotate*

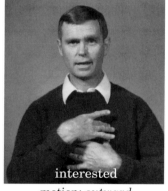

interested

motion: *outward*

in

[the] oral

motion: *circular, sideways*
INITI "O"

and

motion: *l to r*

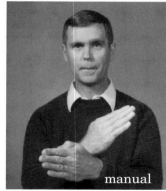

manual

motion: *cross wrists, alternate, slice*

communication

INITI "c"
motion: *back and forth, alternate*

[of the] deaf.

motion: *from ear to mouth*

I [was]

studying

motion: *wiggle finger tips*
option: *add "ing"*

to

option: *fingerspell*

become

motion: *rotate*

a

motion: *sideways (l to r)*

teacher

motion: *short jabs, outward,
then downward*
PICTO: *impart from mind*

[of the]   deaf

[at the] Oregon

motion: *outward in arcs*

school.

motion: *clap*
PICTO: *teacher clapping
hands for students' attention*

[The]   first

motion: *touch*

system

motion: *to the side, then
downward*

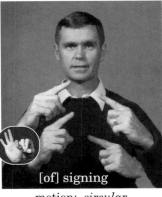

[of] signing

motion: *circular,
alternating, sideways*
option: *add "ing"*

I

learned

motion: *RH upward*

[was] pure

INITI: "p"
motion: *sideways (l to r)*

SEE.
INITI
(<u>S</u>igning <u>E</u>xact <u>E</u>nglish)

I

became
motion: *rotate*

fluent
motion: *outward*
PARA: *"skills"*
ASL type

in

this

method
INITI
motion: *outward*
PARA: *"way"*

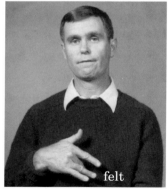

and
motion: *l to r*

felt
motion: *upward*

proud
motion: *upward*

[to be] able
motion: *bend wrists twice*

to
option: *fingerspell*

communicate
INITI
motion: *back and forth,*
alternating

with

deaf
motion: *from ear to mouth*

children

motion: *short arcs to the side*
PICTO: *touch tops of
children's heads*

and

motion: *l to r*

adults

INITI: *"a"*
motion: *downward*
PARA: *"parents"*

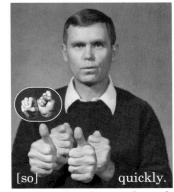

[so]   quickly.

motion: *thumbs out, foward*
option: *add "ly"*

However

PARA: *"but"*
ASL type

[it]   soon

motion: *rub back and forth*
ASL type

became

motion: *rotate*

apparent

PARA: *"obvious" or "clear"*

to

option: *fingerspell*

me

that

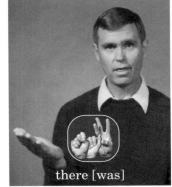

there [was]

motion: *outward*

another

motion: *to the side (l to r)*

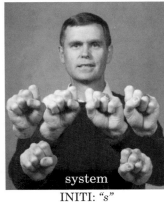

system

INITI: *"s"*
motion: *to the side, then
downward*

being

INITI: *"b"*
motion: *outward*
option: *fingerspell*

used

INITI: *"u"*
motion: *(rh) circular*

by

DACTO

children

motion: *short arcs to the side*
PICTO: *touch tops of
children's heads*

on

[the] playground

motion: *wiggle "y's" then rub
fingertips several times*
PICTO: *"dirt" on playground*

and

motion: *l to r*

in

motion: *outward
follow eye focus*

[the] dorms.

INITI: *"d"*
PARA: *"home"*

I

watched

motion: *short jabs*

this

system

INITI: *"s"*
motion: *to the side, then
downward*

being

INITI: *"b"*
motion: *outward*
option: *fingerspell*

used

INITI: *"u"*
motion: *RH circular,
LH stationary*

from

motion: *RH to the side*

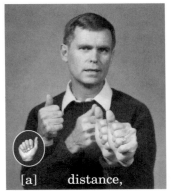

[a] distance,

motion: *RH inward*
PARA: *"far"*

sometimes

motion: *tap palm*

understanding

motion: *flick index*
option: *add "ing"*

some

motion: *slice backwards*

but

mostly

motion: *RH upward*
option: *add "ly"*

understanding

motion: *flick index*
option: *add "ing"*

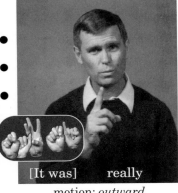

nothing.

motion: *outward or sideways*

[It was] really

motion: *outward*
option: *add "ly"*

very

motion: *to the side*

confusing

motion: *circular, alternating*
COMBO: *"think" + "mix"*
option: *add "ing"*

to

me!

This

other

motion: *to the side*

system

motion: *to the side, then downward*

called

motion: *outward arc*

ASL

DACTO

[did]   not

motion: *outward shake head*

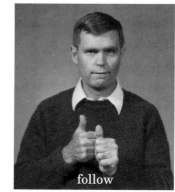

follow

motion: *outward*

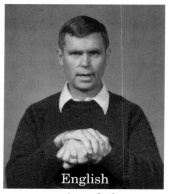

English

motion: *shake*

word

motion: *tap twice*

order.

motion: *l to r*

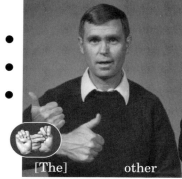

[The]   other

motion: *to the side*

teacher

motion: *outward short jabs then downward for "person" sign*

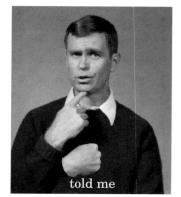

told me

motion: *outward from chin to chest*

that

we

motion: *r to l*

didn't

motion: *to the side*
option: *see above (did not) shake head*

need

motion: *shake vertically*

[to] learn

motion: *upward*

ASL.

[It] would

INITI (SEE borrowing)
motion: *outward*
option: *fingerspell*

not

motion: *outward*

help

motion: *upward*

deaf

children

motion: *short arcs to the side*
PICTO

learn

motion: *upward*

their

motion: *two short jabs
outward*

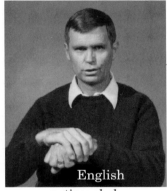

English

motion: *shake*

better!

motion: *to the side, upward*

I

taught

motion: *two short jabs
outward*

deaf

children

motion: *short arcs to the side*
PICTO

for

motion: *outward*

two

years.

motion: *circular, alternating*
PICTO: *the sun and the earth*

I

taught

motion: *two short jabs outward*

speech,

motion: *tap chin twice*
PICTO: *fingers represent words*

reading,

motion: *repeat, up and down*
PICTO: *fingers respresent eyes, flat LH=book*

and

motion: *l to r*

math

INITI
motion: *repeat crossing hands twice*

and

motion: *l to r*

also [was]

motion: *tap side of indexes twice as you move hands to R*

[the] football

motion: *repeat intertwining of fingers.* PICTO: *two teams coming in contact*

and

motion: *l to r*

track

motion: *outward wiggling thumbs*
PARA: *"run"*

coach.

motion: *tap shoulder twice*
PARA: *"boss"* or *"captain"*

All

motion: *RH rotates, then rests upon LH*

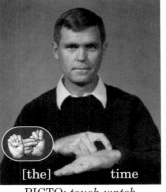

[the]   time

PICTO: *touch watch*

I

used

INITI: *"u"*
motion: *RH circular*

pure

INITI: *"p"*
motion: *to the side*

MCE

DACTO

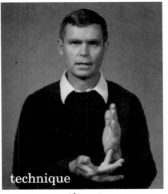

technique

motion: *tap*

with

my

students.

motion: *RH upward, then both hands downward.*

Later

motion: *RH rotates*

after

motion: *RH crosses LH*
PARA: *"across"*

two

more

motion: *fingertips meet*

years

motion: *circular, alternating*

[of]   graduate

INITI: *"g"*
motion: *RH circular, then rest upon LH*

school

motion: *clap twice*

P A U S E

I

started

motion: *twist RH*
PARA: *"began" or "commenced"*

teaching

motion: *two short jabs*
option: *add "ing"*

[at the]   university

INITI: *"u"*
motion: *RH tap LH, then 1/2 circle up*

level

motion: *to the side*

and

motion: *l to r*

established

motion: *RH turn to rest on LH*

[a]   training

INITI: *"t"* / motion: *back and forth* / PARA: *"practice"*
option: *add "ing"*

program

INITI: *"p"*
motion: *RH down palm, then down back of hand*

for

motion: *outward*

teachers

motion: *two shorts jabs outward, then down for "person"*

[of the]   deaf.

I

became

motion: *rotate*

exposed

motion: *palm tap index*
PICTO
ASL type

[to]   more

motion: *fingertips meet*

and

motion: *l to r*

more

motion: *fingertips meet*

ASL

DACTO

through

motion: *slice outward*

my

travels

motion: *circular, to the side*

more

with

[a] theatre

motion: *inward, circular, alternating*

for

motion: *outward*

[the]   deaf

and

motion: *l to r*

summer

motion: *across forehead*

[a]

language

motion: *jiggle as hands separate*

camp.

motion: *hands separate, then downward*
PICTO: *tent poles*

`My

attitude

INITI: *"a"*
motion: *circular on shoulder*

toward

motion: *point, but don't touch*

this

motion: *index tap on palm*

unusual

motion: *to the side*
PARA: *"different'*
note: *lipsynch*

language

INITI: *"l"*
motion: *jiggle hands as hands separate*

began

motion: twist
PARA: *"start"*

[to]   change

motion: *rotate downward*

and

motion: *l to r*

I

began

motion: twist
PARA: *"start"*

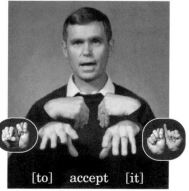

[to]   accept   [it]

motion: *inward*

for

motion: *outward*

[its]   fluidity

motion: *draw thumbs across other fingertips as you move hands outward*

and

motion: *l to r*

theatrical

motion: *alternating, up chest*

qualities.

Fingerspell or INITI
motion: *RH upward*
(suggested by Bragg)

I

thought

motion: *index on temple*

to

motion: *index to index*
option: *fingerspell*

myself

motion: *tap chest twice*

"   "

motion: *bend or wiggle*

what

motion: *RH slice downward*

[a]   fool

motion: *r to l*

I   [was]

for

motion: *outward*

ignoring

motion: *outward*
option: *add "ing"*

what

motion: *RH slice downward*

ASL

DACTO

had

option: *fingerspell*

to

option: *fingerspell*

offer

motion: *outward*
PARA: *"present"*

both

motion: *RH downward*

for

motion: *outward*

[the]   **deaf**

motion: *outward*
follow eye focus

community

motion: *tap fingertips*
twice
PICTO: *tops of roofs*

and

motion: *l to r*

also

motion: *strike sides of*
indexes, separate, repeat,
move to side

for

those

motion: *l to r*

hearing

motion: *small circles*
off mouth
ASL *type*

individuals

INITI: *"i"*
motion: *downward, repeat*
twice, as you move to R

who

motion: *circular,*
around mouth

[are]   interested

motion: *outward*

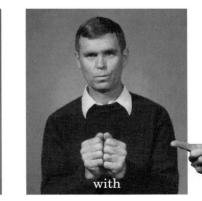

in

working

motion: *tap twice*
option: *add "ing"*

with

them.

motion: *to the side, l to r*

There

motion: *outward*

I

stood

PICTO: *two fingers
represent two legs*

sort of

motion: *rock wrist
ASL type*

like

motion: *tap twice*

[a]   person

motion: *downward*

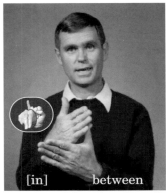

[in]   between

motion: *slide sides of hand
back and forth*

two

cultures —

INITI
motion: *circle index with "c"*

• P A U S E •

[the]   older

motion: *downward off chin,
then upward*

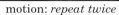

I

became

motion: *rotate*

and

motion: *l to r*

[the]   more

experiences

motion: *repeat twice*

I

had

with

[the]   deaf

motion: *from ear to mouth*

world,

motion: *circular,
alternating, outward*

●
P
A
U
S
E
●

[the]   more

I

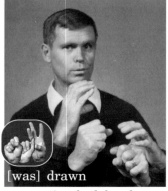

[was] drawn

motion: both hands
close outward—PARA:
"attract" or *"fascinate"*

[to the]   idea

INITI: *"i"*
motion: *upward*

[of] learning

motion: *upward*
option: add *"ing"*

ASL.
DACTO

Then
motion: *right index moves
from thumb to index*

I

met
motion: *two hands meet*

Bernard Bragg.
INITI: (name sign) BB
motion: *small arc
to the side, l to r*

We
motion: *back and forth,
outward
ASL type*

became
motion: *rotate*

good
motion: *upper hand
downward from mouth,
touch lower hand*

friends
motion: *rotate*

and
motion: *l to r*

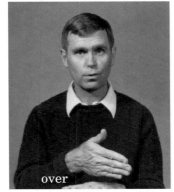

over
motion: *RH crosses LH*
PARA: "across"

many
motion: *repeat twice*

years
motion: *circular, foward*

we
(see above)

developed
INITI: "d"
motion: *upward*

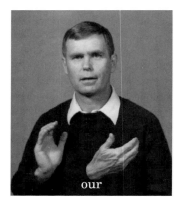

our

own

DACTO

means

INITI: "m"
motion: *outward*
PARA: *"way"*

[of] communication

INITI: "c"
motion: *back and forth,
alternating*

with

each other

motion: *circular,
alternating*

that

combines

motion: *two hands join*

ASL

DACTO

and

motion: *l to r*

English.

motion: *shake*

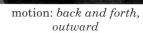

We

motion: *back and forth,
outward*

call

motion: *hands meet,
then outward*

this

mode

motion: *outward*
PARA: *"method" or "means"*

motion: *bend or wiggle*

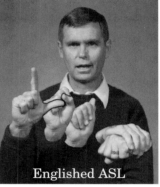

Englished ASL

motion: *l to r*

and

motion: *l to r*

we [are]

motion: *back and forth, sideways*

very

motion: *to the side*

excited

motion: *circular, alternating, inward*

about

motion: *circular, alternating*

using

INITI: "u"
motion: *RH circular*
option: *add "ing"*

[it] with

anyone

INITI: "a"
motion: *"a" turns to "one"*

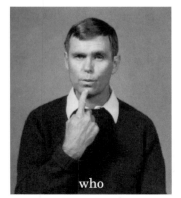

who

motion: *circular, around mouth*

communicates

INITI: "c"
motion: *back and forth*

in

this

language.

INITI: "l"
motion: *jiggle as hands separate*

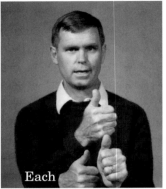

Each

motion: *RH downward twice*

day

motion: *downward*

I

think

that

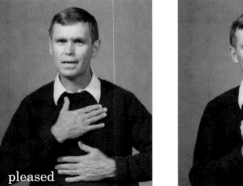

I [am]

becoming

motion: *rotate*
option: *add "ing"*

more

motion: *fingertips meet*

and

motion: *l to r*

more

motion: *fingertips meet*

pleased

motion: *circular, alternating*

with

my

signing

motion: *circular, alternating*
option: *add "ing"*

and

motion: *l to r*

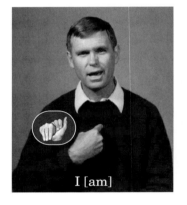

now

motion: *downward*

I

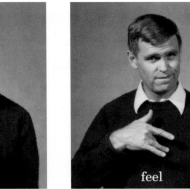

really

motion: *outward*
option: *add "ly"*

feel

motion: *upward*

good

motion: *upperhand moves
down to touch lower hand*

about

motion: *circular,
alternating*

my

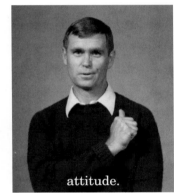

changed

motion: *rotate*
option: *fingerspell*

attitude.

INITI: *"a"*
motion: *circle once, then
to shoulder*

DIALOGUE

Some examples of special signs used in the following dialogue:

PICTO   summer (wipe sweat)
         write (mime)
         book (open the book)
         hearing (words tumble from mouth)
         hand (touch L hand)
         flexible (bend fingers back and forth)

PARA   great = "wonderful"
         get = "arrive"
         a while = "later"
         intimidated = "scared"
         finally = "succeed"
         pretty = "so, so"
         so far = "since"
         just = "only," "simply"
         track = "way"
         valuable = "important"
         appreciate = "enjoy," "please"
         into = "enter"
         way = "method"
         discovered = "found"
         disparate = "opposite"
         native = "national," "natural"
         gone through = "finish"
         a lot = "much"
         compromising = "agree"
         represents = "show"
         should = "must"
         well = "good"
         else = "other"
         adjust = "change," "adapt"

DACTO   order

COMBO   learn (book + mind), home (food + bed)

INITI   **m**iddle, **r**oad, **c**oncepts, **n**ative, **c**ompromising, **B**ozeman, **n**ational, **w**orkshop, **t**otal communication, **c**hance, **v**isits, **p**hilosophy, **f**oreign, **c**ould, **p**arents, **s**ystems, **b**ackgrounds, language, **v**isualness, etc.

ASL
SIGNS: let's see
         we
         didn't
         do do (idiom)
         deaf
         each other
         nil
         ?
         hearing person
         built up
         courage
         back then
         has resulted in (finish)
         have (finish)
         lousy
         read
         so far
         started out
         incorporate
         loud
         English

DIALOGUE

Bernard Bragg and Jack Olson

BB: Jack (name sign), it's great to be here in Bozeman again!

JO: Let's see, this is about your 10th trip out here, right?

BB: I can still remember that first summer when I taught at the National Workshop in Total Communication. We didn't have the chance to really know each other during my first visit.

JO: I know, I think that I was a bit shy. I watched you from a distance. My ASL skills were nil. I think you really intimidated me.

BB: What happened? How did we finally get to know each other?

JO: Well, it took a while, but later I built up my courage to introduce myself and then we discovered we had things in common.

BB: Your signing back then was pretty lousy, but you've really made some progress. I wish you could read fingerspelling better.

JO: I know, but I think I'm improving, right?

BB: Right (fingerspell).

JO: What? Understand?

BB: Quit acting! That's my line.

JO: Are you telling me? We've come a long way since we started writing. Say, how many changes have we made on our book so far?

BB: I lost count. Just to think we started out to write just another sign dictionary!

JO: And how many of those have been published?

BB: I think..I hope...we're on the right track focusing mostly on the linguistic philosophy.

JO: What has led us to this idea for our book is my resistance to accepting ASL at the beginning. It seemed so foreign! But my work with my theater gave me some valuable insights.

BB: Then you had a change of attitude?

JO: I guess you could say that. We were trying to please everyone who came to our performances. Hearing parents wanted SEE. Deaf people wanted ASL. It was frustrating trying to put a show together!

BB: So, what did you do then?

JO: I invited an ASL consultant to help and we started to use both systems.

BB: (tongue in cheek) Signing SEE with one hand and ASL with the other hand?

JO: Oh, BB—come on! I simply learned to be more flexible.

BB: Sure, you just began to appreciate ASL more and tried to incorporate it into your show. Right?

JO: Then I realized that there must be a different way of communicating with sign language. I think we have discovered it!

BB: Thanks to our disparate backgrounds! You first learned SEE because you thought that it was the only proper language to communicate with.

JO: But now, I really do appreciate ASL and can see how its visualness helps to make concepts much more clear.

BB: And loud?

JO: You bet! You're a native signer who has gone through a lot to learn English.

BB: Our friendship has resulted in a more compromising way of communicating with each other. Well, we've met halfway!

JO: Our book represents "the middle of the road" perspective—and it should work as well for everybody else.

BB: Jack, we are at peace with each other and at home with anyone else who is willing to adjust in order to communicate better.

JO: Amen!

Jack,

INITI: <u>J</u>ack
"name sign"—"J" scratched
on chest

[It is]   great

motion: *outward*
PARA: "wonderful"
(palms out)

[to be]   here

motion: *small opposing
circle; palms out*

in

Bozeman

INITI: "B"
motion: *make a "z" with
"b" handshape*

again.

motion: *RH tap on palm*

Let's see,

motion: *tap on cheek twice
ASL type*

this

motion: *index tap palm*

[is]   about

motion: *circle RH index
around LH index*

your

motion: *outward*

tenth

motion: *shake fist back and
forth add "th"*

trip,

motion: *outward small,
alternating circles*

P A U S E

right?

motion: *strike fists
ASL type: "?" on face*

I

can

motion: *downward*

still

motion: *outward*

remember

motion: *thumbs meet*

that

first

motion: *strike finger
against thumb*

summer

motion: *l to r*
PICTO: *imagine
wiping sweat*

when

motion: *small circle RH
before fingers touch*

I

taught

motion: *two short jabs
outward*
PICTO: *info from mind*

[at the]   National

INITI: "n"
motion: *1/2 circle,
then touch*

Workshop

INITI: "w" and "s"
motion: *outward*

in

Total Communication.

INITI: "t" and "c"
motion: *"t" moves back and
forth alternating with "c"*

We

motion: *back and forth
ASL type*

didn't

motion: *under chin, then out
ASL type*

have

[the] chance

INITI: "c"
motion: *hands turn down-
ward.* PARA: *"happen"*

[to] really

motion: *outward*
option: *add "ly"*

know

motion: *tap on
forehead twice*

each other

motion: *alternating circles*
PARA: *"assoicate"*
ASL type

during

motion: *outward*

my

first

motion: *finger hit thumb*

visit.

INITI: "v"
motion: *alternating small
circles*

I

know

motion: *tap on
forehead twice*

I

think

that

I [was a]

bit

motion: *flick thumb twice*

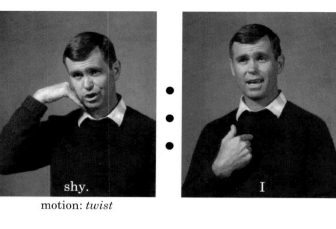

shy.
motion: *twist*

I

watched
motion: *short jabs; fingers
represent eyes*
PICTO

you

from
motion: *RH to right*

afar.
motion: *LH inward*

My

ASL
DACTO

skills　[were]

nil.
motion: *hit palm*
ASL type

I

think
motion: *nod head*
ASL type

you
motion: *outward*

really
option: *add "ly"*

intimidated
motion: *toward chest*
PARA: *"scared"* or
"frightened"

me.

What

motion: *index finger slices all others*

happened?

motion: *twist downward*
ASL type: *"?" on face*

PAUSE

How

motion: *twist outward*

[did]   we

motion: *back and forth*
ASL type

finally

PARA: *"succeed"*
option: *add "ly"*

get

motion: *tap on palm*
PARA: *"arrive" or "become"*

[to]   know

motion: *tap forehead*

each other?

motion: *alternating circles*
ASL type

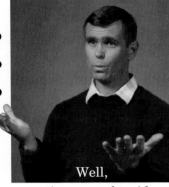

Well,

motion: *expand to side*

[it]   took

motion: *inward*

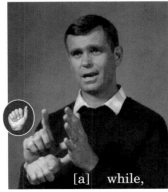

[a]   while,

PARA: *"later"*
ASL type

but

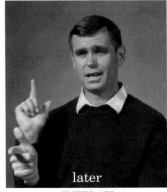

later

INITI: *"l"*
motion: *outward*

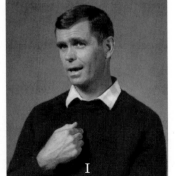

I

built up

motion: *upward, alternating*

my

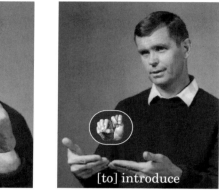

courage

motion: *outward*

[to] introduce

motion: *both hands meet*

myself

motion: *tap chest twice*

and

motion: *l to r*

then

motion: *strike thumb, then index*

we

motion: *back and forth ASL type*

discovered

motion: *RH upward* PARA: *"found"*

we

motion: *back and forth ASL type*

had

motion: *to chest*

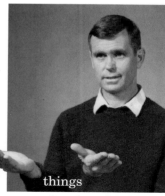

things

motion: *l to r in arc, palm up*

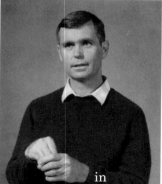

in

common.

motion: *back and forth, repeat* option: *fingerspell*

Your

motion: *outward*

95

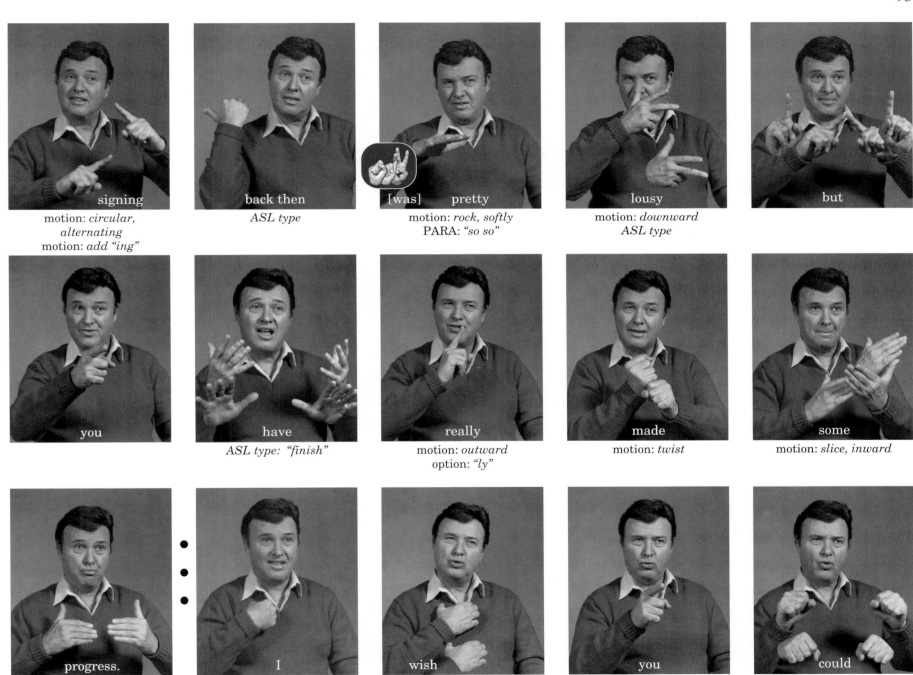

signing
motion: *circular,*
alternating
motion: *add "ing"*

back then
ASL type

[was]   pretty
motion: *rock, softly*
PARA: "so so"

lousy
motion: *downward*
ASL type

but

you

have
ASL type: "finish"

really
motion: *outward*
option: "ly"

made
motion: *twist*

some
motion: *slice, inward*

progress.
motion: *outward,*
alternating

I

wish
motion: *downward*

you

could
motion: *downward*
Note: *lipsynch*

read

ASL type

fingerspelling

motion: *l to r*

better.

motion: *upward*

I

know,

motion: *tap forehead twice*

but

I

think

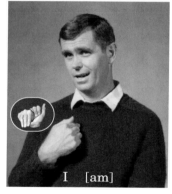

I   [am]

improving,

motion: *chop frequently*
up arm
option: add *"ing"*

right?

motion: *strike hands to-*
gether, nod head
ASL: *"?" on face*

"r....g....t" !

motion: *"right" spelled*
rapidly on purpose

What?

motion: *index finger*
brush LH
ASL: *A big "?" on face*

PAUSE

Understand?

motion: *head shake*
ASL type

Quit

motion: *strike downward*
PARA: *"stop"*

acting,

motion: *circular, alternating, inward*

that's

option: *twist fist for "s"*

my

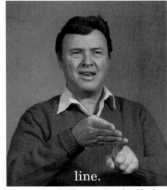

line.

motion: *RH outward all the way across the lower finger*
PARA: *"major" or "field"*

[Are] you

• • •

telling me?

motion: *from chin to chest*
ASL type
ASL: *"?" on face*

• P A U S E •

We

motion: *back and forth, repeat*
ASL type

have

ASL type: *"finish"*

come

motion: *circular, alternating toward chest*

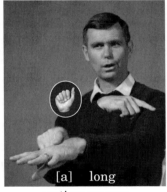

[a] long

motion: *up arm*

way

INITI: *"w"*
motion: *outward*

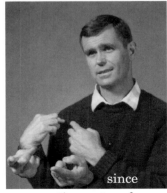

since

motion: *outward*

we

motion: *back and forth, repeat*
ASL type

started

motion: *twist finger*

writing.

motion: *scribble across palm*
PICTO
option: *add "ing"*

• P A U S E •

Say,

motion: *off chin to chest*
ASL type

how

motion: *palms down,
then up*

many

motion: *upward*

changes

motion: *twist*

have

ASL "finish"

we

motion: *back and forth*
ASL type

made

motion: *twist*

on

our

motion: *r to l across chest*

book

PICTO: *open a book*

so far?

PARA: "since"
ASL: "?" on face

I

lost

motion: *downward*
ASL: "can't"

count.

motion: *slide upward
across palm*

● P A U S E ●

Just

motion: *twist*
PARA: "only"

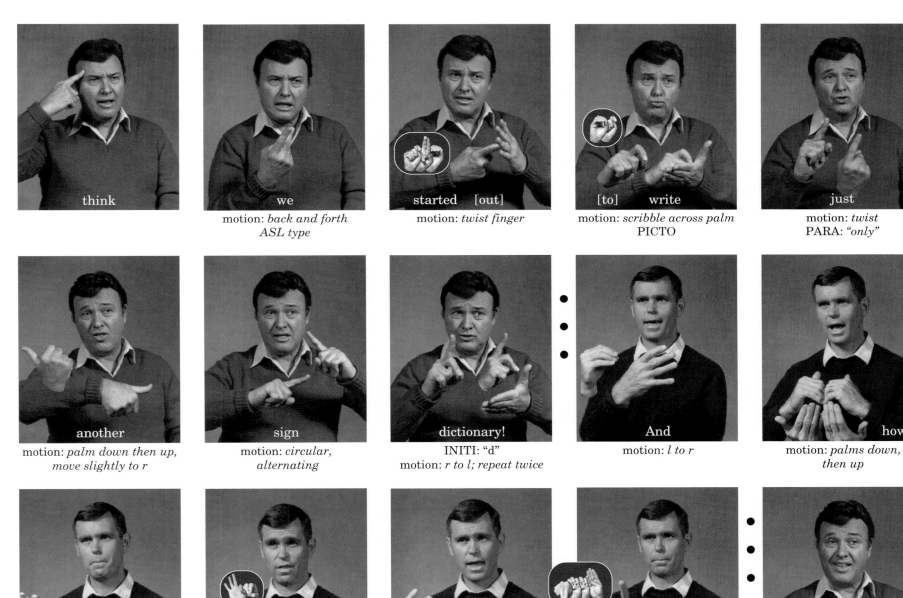

think	we	started [out]	[to] write	just
	motion: *back and forth* / ASL type	motion: *twist finger*	motion: *scribble across palm* / PICTO	motion: *twist* / PARA: *"only"*

another	sign	dictionary!	And	how
motion: *palm down then up, move slightly to r*	motion: *circular, alternating*	INITI: "d" / motion: *r to l; repeat twice*	motion: *l to r*	motion: *palms down, then up*

many	[of] those	have	[been] published?	I
motion: *upward*	motion: *pointing l to r*	ASL: *"finish"*	motion: *RH tap on palm* / ASL type: *"?" on face*	

think

I

hope

motion: *flutter both hands*

we   [are]

motion: *back and forth, repeat*
ASL type

on

[the]   right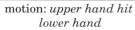

motion: *upper hand hit lower hand*

track

motion: *outward*
PARA: *"way"* or *"method"*

focusing

motion: *twist*
option: *add "ing"*

mostly

motion: *RH upward*
option: *add "ly"*

on

[the]   linguistic

INITI: *"l"*
motion: *to the side*
PARA: *"language"*

philsophy.

INITI: *"p"*
motion: *small up and down, repeat*

What

motion: *slice across fingers*

has

ASL *"finish"*

led

motion: *outward*

us

motion: *back and forth, repeat*
PARA: "we"--- ASL type

[to]   this

motion: *index tap on palm*

idea

motion: *outward*

for

motion: *outward*

our

motion: *r to l*

book

PICTO: *open a book*

[is]   my

resistance

motion: *outward jab of elbow, repeat twice*
ASL type

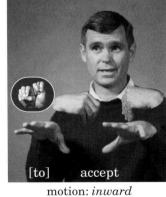

[to]   accept

motion: *inward*

ASL

DACTO

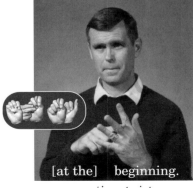

[at the]   beginning.

motion: *twist*
PARA: "start"

● P A U S E ●

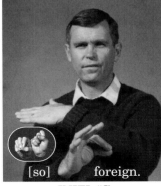

[It]   seemed

motion: *twist*

[so]   foreign.

INITI: "f"
motion: *circle "f" on elbow*

But

my

work

motion: *tap twice on wrist*

with

my

theatre

INITI: "t"
motion: *circular, alternating*

gave

motion: *toward chest*
ASL type: *directional*

me

some

motion: *slice toward body*

valuable

INITI: "v"
motion: *circle upward, touch*
PARA: "important"

insights.

motion: *RH outward, then under LH*
PARA: "outlook"

Then

motion: *strike thumb, then index*

you

had

motion: *tap on chest*

[a]   change

motion: *rotate*

[of]   attitude?

INITI: "a"
motion: *small circle on chest*
ASL type: "?" *on face*

I

guess

motion: *downward*
mime: *"grasp"*

you

could

motion: *downward*
PARA: *"can"*

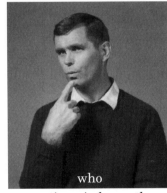

say

motion: *small arc
from mouth*

that.

• P A U S E •

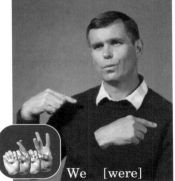

We   [were]

motion: *r shoulder to l
shoulder*

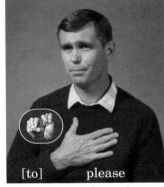

trying

INITI: *"t"*
motion: *outward*
option: *add "ing"*

[to]   please

motion: *circle on chest,
clockwise*

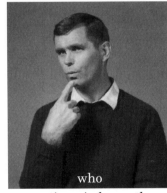

everyone

motion: *slide RH down l,
then up and out*

who

motion: *circle mouth*

came

motion: *alternating circles
inward. Tense is understood
by context.*

[to]   our

motion: *r shoulder to
l shoulder*

performances.

motion: *alternating circles
toward chest.*
Note: *lipsynch*

• P A U S E •

Hearing

motion: *small outward
circles from mouth*
PICTO: *words from mouth*

parents

INITI: *"p"*
motion: *downward*
PARA: *mother, father*

wanted
*motion: inward
(tense by context)*

SEE.
DACTO
<u>S</u>igning <u>E</u>xact <u>E</u>nglish

• **PAUSE** •

Deaf
motion: ear to mouth

people
*motion: outward, circular,
alternating*

wanted
*motion: inward
(tense by context)*

• **PAUSE** •

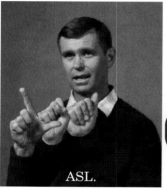

ASL.
DACTO

[It was]   frustrating
*motion: tap under chin
with back of RH*

trying   [to]
*motion: outward
option: add "ing"*

put together
*motion: interlocking of
fingers as in "gear" action
ASL type*

[a]   show.
*motion: circular,
alternating*

[So]   what
motion: slice across fingers

[did]   you

do
ASL idiom: "do, do"

then?
*motion: strike thumb
then index
ASL: "?" on face*

I

hired

motion: *from r side inward*

[an] ASL

DACTO

consultant

motion: *strike wrist with RH "O" then open to a "5" palm outward*

[to] help

motion: *upward*

and

motion: *l ? r*

we

motion: *r shoulder to l shoulder*

started

motion: *twist index*

[to] use

INITI: "u"
motion: *small circular*

both

motion: *RH downward*

systems.

INITI: "s"
motion: *separate fists, then downward*

Signing

motion: *circular, alternating*
option: *add "ing"*

SEE

DACTO

with

one

hand

motion: *touch L hand*

and

motion: *l to r*

signing

motion: *circular, alternating*
option: *add "ing"*

ASL

DACTO

with

[the]   other

motion: *to the right*

hand

motion: *touch R hand*

?

motion: *wiggle index*

[Oh,] come on!

motion: *r to l*

**P
A
U
S
E**

I

simply

motion: *palm out,
then in, twist*
PARA: *"only" or "just"*

learned

motion: *from palm to
forehead*—PICTO: *info from
book to mind*

[to be]   more

motion: *fingertips meet*

flexible.

motion: *grasp fingertips,
bend back and forth*
PICTO

Sure,

motion: *outward*

you

just

motion: *twist*
PARA: *"only"*
Note: *lipsynch*

began   [to]

motion: *twist index*

apprecoate

motion: *alternating circles*
PARA: *"enjoy"*
Note: *lipsynch*

ASL

DACTO

more

motion: *fingertips meet*

and

motion: *l to r*

tried

INITI: *"t"*
motion: *outward*

[to] incorporate

motion: *downward*
PICTO: *think of gears
meshing*—PARA: *"machine"*

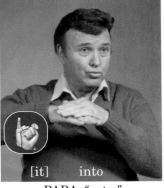

[it]   into

PARA: *"enter"*
ASL type

your

motion: *outward*

show,

motion: *circular,
alternating*

● P A U S E ●

right?

motion: *strike hands*
ASL type: *"?" on face*

●
●
●

Then

motion: *strike thumb
then index*

I

realized

motion: *small circles*

that

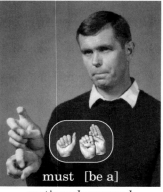

there

motion: *outward*

must   [be a]

motion: *downward*
PARA: *"need" or "should"*

different

motion: *to the side*

way

INITI: "w"
motion: *outward*

[of] communicating

INITI: "c"
motion: *back and forth,
alternating*

with

sign

motion: *circular,
alternating*

language.

INITI: "l"
motion: *thumbs almost meet,
then separate*

● P A U S E ●

I

think

we

motion: *back and forth
ASL type*

have

ASL: *"finish"*

discovered   [it!]

motion: *RH upward*

●
●
●

Thanks

motion: *outward*

to

option: fingerspell

our

motion: r to l

disparate

PARA: *"opposite"*

backgrounds!

INITI: *"b" and "g"*
motion: downward

● **P A U S E** ●

You

first

learned

motion: from palm to
forehead—PITCO: info from
book to mind

SEE

DACTO

because

motion: RH to the side,
then upward

You

you

thought

motion: head nod

that [it was]

[the] only

motion: palm out, then in

proper

motion: tap twice

language

INITI: *"l"*
motion: to the side

you

[to] communicate

INITI: "c"
motion: *alternate "c's"*
back and forth

with.

But

now

motion: *downward*

I

really

motion: *downward*
option: *add "ly"*

[do]   appreciate

motion: *circular, clockwise*

ASL

DACTO

and

can

motion: *downward*

see

motion: *outward*

how

motion: *palm in, then*
palm out

[its]   visualness

INITI: <u>v</u> = motion: *outward*
<u>n</u> = motion: *downward*
(borrowed from SEE)

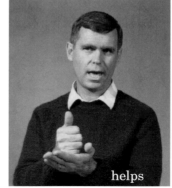

helps

motion: *upward*

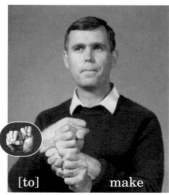

[to]   make

motion: *twist*

concepts
INITI: "i"
motion: *outward*

much
motion: *to the side*

more
motion: *fingertips meet*

clear.
motion: *l to r*

And

loud
motion: *shake fists*
ASL type

?
motion: *wiggle*
ASL type: "?" on face

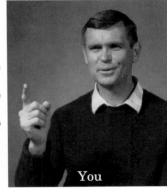

You

bet!
motion: *palms up, palms
down*—PICTO: *slapping
cards on table*

PAUSE

You [are]

[a]   native
INITI: "n"
motion: *small circle
downward (lipsynch)*

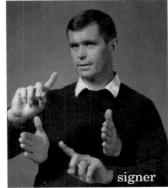

signer
motion: *circular,
alternating plus downward
movement for "person" sign*

who
motion: *around mouth*

has
ASL: *"finish"*

gone
motion: *outward*

through

motion: *outward*

[a] lot

motion: *to the side*
PARA: *"much"*

[to] learn

motion: *upward*

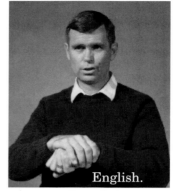

English.

motion: *shake*

Our

motion: *r to l*

friendship

motion: *index fingers
alternate*

has

ASL: *"finish"*

resulted

INITI: "r"
motion: *downward*

in

 *(right position: [a] more)*

[a] more

motion: *fingertips meet*

compromising

INITI: "c"
COMBO: *"think"* + *"same"*
PARA: *"agree"*

way

motion: *outward*

[of] communicating

INITI: "c"
motion: *back and forth
alternating*

with

each other.

motion: *circular,
alternating*

P
A
U
S
E

Well,

motion: *upward and out*

we

motion: *back and forth*
ASL type

have

ASL: *"finish"*

met

half

motion: *slice finger index*

way!

motion: *outward*

Our

motion: *r to l*

book

PICTO: *open a book*

represents

INITI: *"r"*
motion: *outward*
PARA: *"show"*

"   "

motion: *twist or wiggle*

[the]   middle

motion: *small circle,*
then touch palm

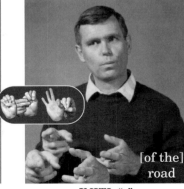

[of the] road

INITI: *"r"*
motion: *outward*
PARA: *"way"*

perspective

motion: *from cheek to index*
PARA: *"point of view"*

and

motion: *l to r*

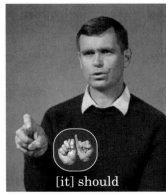

[it] should

motion: *downward*
PARA: *"must" or "need"*
Note: *lipsynch*

work

motion: *tap twice*

as

motion: *l to r*

well

motion: *downward*
PARA: *"good"*
Note: *lipsynch*

for

motion: *outward*

everyone

motion: *RH downward LH
twice, then index finger
sweeping from l to r*

else.

motion: *l to r*
PARA: *"other"*

Jack,

INITI: *"j"*
motion: *scratch "j" on chest*

we [are]

motion: *back and forth
ASL type*

[at]   peace

motion: *alternate clasping
of hands*

with

each other

motion: *circular,
alternating*

and

motion: *l to r*

[at]   home

motion: *inward*
COMBO: *"food" + "bed"*

with

anyone else

motion: *"a" l to r; index
sweeping; "a" arc to right*

who [is]

motion: *around mouth*

willing

motion: *outward*

[to] adjust

motion: *twist*
PARA: *"change"*

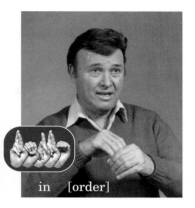

in [order]

[to] communicate

INITI: "c"
motion: *back and forth*

better!

motion: *l to r, then upward*

AMEN!

motion: *RH tap on palm*

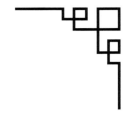
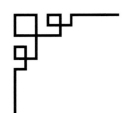
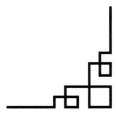
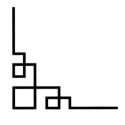

"STOPPING BY WOODS ON A SNOWY EVENING"

(Sign Mime Translation)

STOPPING BY WOODS ON A SNOWY EVENING

Robert Frost

Whose woods these are I think I know.
His house is in the village though;
He will not see me stopping here
To watch his woods fill up with snow.

My little horse must think it queer
To stop without a farmhouse near
Between the woods and frozen lake
The darkest evening of the year.

He gives his harness bells a shake
To ask if there is some mistake.
The only other sound's the sweep
Of easy wind and downy flake.

The woods are lovely, dark and deep,
But I have promises to keep,
And miles to go before I sleep,
And miles to go before I sleep.

STOPPING BY WOODS ON A SNOWY EVENING

Robert Frost

Translation by Bernard Bragg
(Signs shown here are static, but actually they
are meant to move through space.)

Whose

woods

these are

I think

I know.

His

house

is (in)

(the) village

though;

He · will · not · see me · (stoppping) · here

(To) watch his · woods · white · snow · fill up

fill up with snow.

My · little · horse · (must) think · (it) queer

(To) stop

without

(a) farmhouse

near

Between

(the) woods

"water"

"ice"

(and) frozen lake.

(The) darkest

evening

"during"

(of the)

year.

He

(give his harness)

(bells a shake)

(To ask)

if

there (is some) mistake.

(The) only

other sound('s)

(the) sweep

(Of) easy wind

(and) downy flake.

(The) woods

(are) lovely,

dark

(and) deep,

But

I

have

promises

"hold"
(to) keep,

And   miles   (to) go

before   I sleep,

And   miles   (to) go

before   I sleep.

STOPPING BY WOODS ON A SNOWY EVENING

Technical Description of Sign Mime Translation

POEM	MOTION	TYPE	OTHER
"Whose"	index circles mouth, LH palm outward		question on face/eyes
"woods"	sweep with fluttering LH to the right (outline trees)	PICTO	
"these are"	sweep with RH out to the right		
"I think"	2 words, 2 signs at once		eye focus down (pausing to reflect)
"I know"	2 words, 2 signs at once		
"His"	RH outward		eyes move to the right
"house"	outline the shape of a house (roof, walls)	PICTO	
"is in"	2 words, 2 signs at once		
"the village"	tap fingertips twice moving entire procedure in a circle, representing the roofs of houses	PICTO	
"though"	rock "y" handshape	ASL "yes"	
"He"	point		
"will"	RH outward		

POEM	MOTION	TYPE	OTHER
"not"	cross hands, separate		
"see me"	two words, two signs—point to self	ASL directional verb	
"stopping"	mime tugging at reins		
"here"	both hands circular		eye focus up
"To watch his woods"			note eye focus
"fill up with snow"	flutter fingertips RH LH depicts tree RH depicts falling snow RH moves up tree to show increase in snow level		
"My"	point		change of eye focus
"little"	two rapid small movements of hands (natural gesture) to indicate size		
"horse"		PICTO (ears)	
"must think"	LH (over there)		
"it queer"	"y" handshape refers to horse "c" handshape moves across face (queer)		
"To stop"		standard sign	
"without"		standard sign	
"a farmhouse"	LH indicates position of house	standard signs	
"near"		standard signs	change of eye focus

POEM	MOTION	TYPE	OTHER
"Between"		standard sign	change of eye focus
"the woods"		standard sign	change of eye focus
"and frozen lake"	water represented by RH . . . . the water's surface LH moves to L as you flutter fingertips, ... then fingers tense	distant ASL type, adjective follows	
"the darkest"		standard sign	
"evening"		standard sign	
"of"	outward	PARA "during"	
"the year."		standard sign	
"He"	LH points (refers to horse)	close-up	change in eye focus
"gives"	mime action (signer becomes horse)		
"his harness bells a shake"		mime action	
"To ask"			eye focus back toward driver
"if"	alternate, up and down	standard sign	
"there is some mistake" . .	1 photo, 2 signs		
"The only"	palm out, palm in	standard sign	
"other sound's"	note flow of hands		

POEM	MOTION	TYPE	OTHER
"the sweep"	R to L		
"Of easy wind"	sweep back and forth	PARA: "light"	signer reflects
"and downy flake"	small outward arc (downy) flutter fingertips (flake)	PARA: "delicate"	eyes follow flakes as they fall
"The woods"			change of eye focus
"are lovely,"	RH (beautiful) LH (woods)	PARA: "beautiful"	
"dark"		standard sign	
"and deep"	RH passes LH	linear "deep"	eyes follow sign
"But"		standard sign	change of eye focus
"I"			change of eye focus, reflects
"have"		standard sign	
"promises"		standard sign	
"to keep,"		ASL type PARA: "hold"	
"And"		standard sign	
"miles"		invented sign based on "measure"	
"to go"		ASL, directional	
"before"		standard sign	
"I sleep,"	note "I" to chest	standard sign	

Stopping by Woods on a Snowy Evening,

Robert Frost

An Interview with Bernard Bragg

JO: Why do you like this poem?

BB: This poem easily lends itself to sign and mime. I have a common and strong identity with R. Frost's experiences. He is sharing his common and emotional experiences with his readers. All we need to do is to stop and appreciate the world around us to understand this poem.

JO: What special techniques do you use when you interpret this poem?

BB: I use the *cinematic technique*—that is, as I sign, I may go from long to short to close-up shots. This is also called visual vernacular. For example, in Frost's poem you will see me create the *trees* from a distance, then you will follow the direction of my eyes for a "close up" of the same trees. Afterwards, I will *cut* to the horse, then cut to the forest, then to the snow. The poses I create here for the reader/viewer are really still/frozen pictures—something I would not use on the *live* stage—but the feeling is still there.

JO: How can the intermediate signer best prepare himself/herself for this poetic interpreting experience?

BB: The signer should try to grasp the *picture* or *image* suggested by the poem, then experiment with conceptual signs to fit the images you see. Remember, words only suggest, *you* must bring to the words your own experiences. For example, it is a paradox that through my eyes and movements you can *see* Frost's poem. His words become written all over my face, hands, and body.

JO: Have you ever had any special experiences that would make you better able to appreciate this piece by Frost?

BB: No particular specific experience as Frost describes in this poem—rather, I am able to generalize to many different life experiences that help me to get the right *feel* and *set* for this piece—such as the beauty of nature in general—it's everywhere, everyplace in the world; not just on a snowy country road in the middle of winter, etc. I draw on memories of places I've been all over the world. I've had the same feeling when I was on the ocean in a boat—the brilliant sun, the sparkling blue of the water—a lone bird silhouetted against the sky. I could say "the sky is lovely, clear and deep, but I have promises to keep....." It's the same emotional experience that I can conjure up in Frost's poem. Some groups may approach this poem differently and attempt to attach other meanings, other interpretations. They might say that this poem is Frost's *death wish* because he says," I have many miles to go before I sleep," but I don't see it that way.

JO: What other advice would you give aesthetic signers about selecting appropriate pieces to interpret?

BB: There are thousands of poems to be *discovered*. Read as many as you can—find those which hit your chord. You must feel a piece deeply enough to really want to share it with others. Give it *life* with animation and feeling through conceptual sign and mime.

JO: What other experiences have you had that make you love literature so much? Deaf people usually are not so good with the printed word.

BB: Robert Panara, my first deaf teacher—he was the door. He gave me the inspiration to break down the barriers of not being able to *hear* the language. I think that I was born with a great passion for the language. People have different skills, aptitudes, knacks—mine was with language. Because of my deafness, I cannot easily get to the words the same way as you (juxtaposition). Somehow, I had to break the barrier and get to those words through imagination—through the *mind's ear*. Bob Panara came along and opened my mind, or rather my eyes.

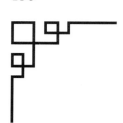

DEATH

(An ASL Poem)

Bernard Bragg

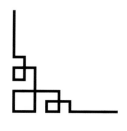

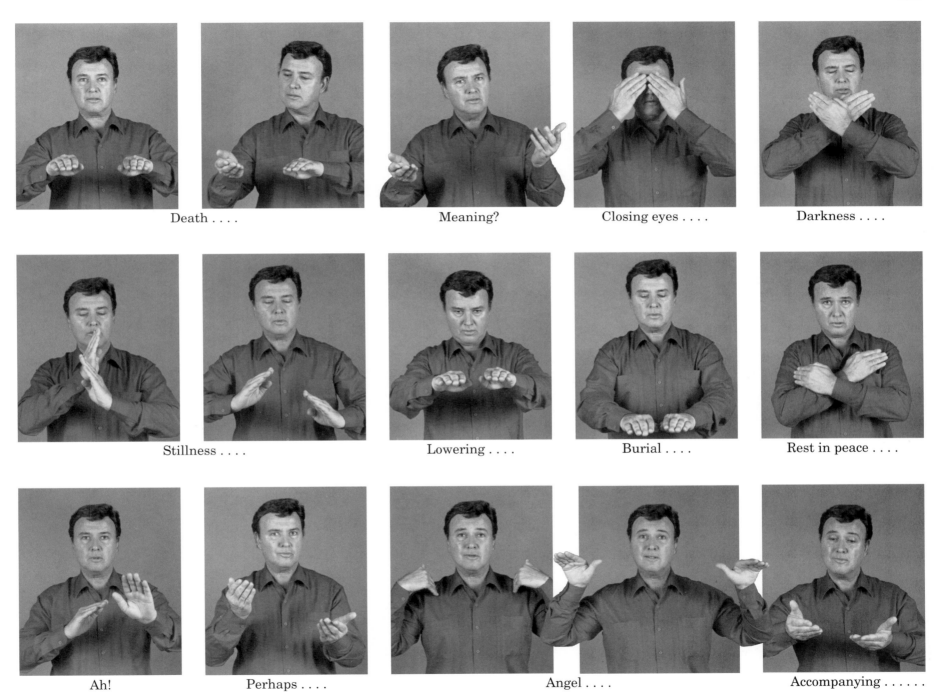

Death . . . .

Meaning?

Closing eyes . . . .

Darkness . . . .

Stillness . . . .

Lowering . . . .

Burial . . . .

Rest in peace . . . .

Ah!

Perhaps . . . .

Angel . . . .

Accompanying . . . . . .

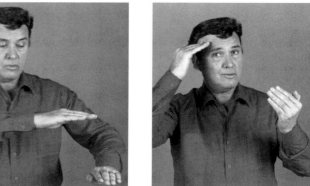

. . . .

Heavenward . . . .

Before Supreme Power?

Or . . . .

Maybe . . . .

Downward . . . .

Entering below . . . .

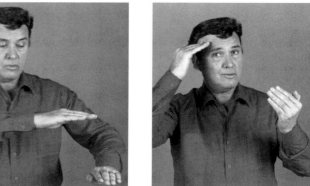

Unknowing . . . .

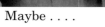 . . . .

Waiting . . . .

Hoping . . . .

DEATH

DIALOGUE ABOUT AN ASL POEM

Bernard Bragg and Jack Olson

JO: Tell me about ASL poetry—it is new—how did it get started?

BB: Oh, it's not new—it's been around for as long as I can remember. I can still see my father using it on stage—a poem presented in the ASL manner. That was many years ago. He never did give it a name, though.

JO: So, how is it different from sign mime?

BB: In ASL poetry, there is an "alliteration" of sign. The hand shape becomes the "rhyme" of sign. The ASL elements are unique and are a very important part of deaf culture. In order for ASL to stay alive, it must have its own poetry—its own unique contribution to deaf culture.

JO: Are you saying there are no set rules?

BB: Only that the handshape(s) remain constant—the rest is invented and up to the imagination of the signers.

JO: Is there anything else that we should be aware of concerning ASL poetry.

BB: Yes. ASL poetry is a most unusual art form involving hand movement and hand shape in an exacting and flowing manner to convey the mood and emotion of the piece. It is a condensed sign technique that focuses on sign simplicity and economy of movement. It cannot be appreciated written down on paper—rather it must be seen as a "visual-spatial" poetry.

JO: When did you write your ASL poem "Death?"

BB: Four years ago.

JO: How does ASL poetry apply to our approach?

BB: It gives us even a better appreciation of ASL technique. Because the signer is limited to basic handshapes at most, he or she must rely upon his or her body and face to tell most of the story. The generic handshape that is used throughout this piece is the "open hand." For some of the concepts the fingers may open slightly or they may bend.

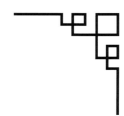

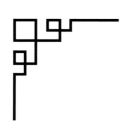

EXERCISES

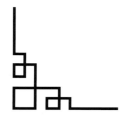

Exercise #1: Signs for Consideration

(To be used for class discussion/analysis of the Visual Spatial Communication technique)

There are no photos used for this exercise or for the other exercises/stories. Students are encouraged to follow the directions given and as a group **create** the signs listed below. In some instances, there may be actual regional signs already in use for some of these signs, but the authors predict that most are new and therefore the visual spatial concept for each needs to be **invented**. The need to invent visual spatial concepts for signs is nothing new—after all, that is how sign language was probably created in the first place!

Divide your class up into groups and first work with the "target signs." Think through the concepts and the suggested motions. If you get stuck, be sure to ask your qualified native signer or teacher. Don't be afraid to experiment. Perhaps your group will decide that there is a better way to **sign** one of the five target signs. Afterwards, move on the list of words following. Be sure to thoroughly analyze and discuss each with your particular group. Your teacher may want you to present your newly created visual spatial concepts before the entire class. The interchange among the several groups should help everyone better relate to the five categories utilized in the method used for this book.

Target Sign	Possible Concept	Motion	Type
1. space shuttle	rockets, piggy back, separate	upward, both hands	PICTO-like
2. conducive	help	upward, both hands	INITI, PARA
3. ecology	animal, environment	combine the two standard signs	COMBO
4. Klu Klux Klan	hooded man	K's outline hood	INITI-PICTO
5. software	computer, program	combine both standard signs	COMBO-PARA

These five signs concepts as well as those that follow should all be part of our cultural literacy.

Now that you have thoroughly discussed and analyzed the five target signs, proceed with the following list of words that need visual spatial concepts created for them according to the five categories outlined before.

1. overdraft
2. dyslexia
3. gospel (song)
4. aphrodisiac
5. malignancy
6. procrastinate
7. glut
8. risqué
9. status quo

10. facade
11. ritual
12. schmaltzy
13. yuppies
14. sexist
15. refugee
16. monopoly
17. mania
18. libel

19. Pegasus
20. Utopia
21. AIDS
22. terrorism
23. manic depressive
24. overdraft (checking)
25. cult
26. macho

For additional practice, each group could select more concepts for analysis and later discussion. A good source:

CULTURAL LITERACY,
What Every American Needs to Know,
by E.D. Hirsch, Jr.,
Random House (Vintage Books)
ISBN 0-394-75843-9 (pbk.)

Exercise #2: Student Exercises Sign

1. Discuss the concepts for using the terms: (1) PARA, (2) PICTO, (3) DACTO, (4) COMBO, and (5) INITI signs.

Students should use an example of each in a sentence and present their work to the class. The class can discuss each presentation and start to use these categories of signs daily.

2. Each student should create a short scenario for class presentation that includes all 5 of the above categories. Here are some possible topics. Be sure to include any ASL principles that you can think of for the following story.

a.	My Grandfather	c.	A First Kiss
b.	Learning to Ski	d.	An Unforgettable Experience

For example:"I learned to ski on terrible equipment—long stiff skis and clamp bindings, under poor snow conditions—heavy, wet, Oregon, snow, and with little or no encouragement from my friends. How I managed to **not** break a limb I will never know! I have fallen at least 5 times in every possible position including a somersault into a snow bank, and falling over backwards into the splits! My friends laughed at me and said, "You'll never be a skier!" Little did I know that one day I would be the father of an Olympic skier and three-time U.S. National Downhill Champion. I even got "good enough" eventually to ski with him. I don't try to keep up, rather we ride the chair lift together and then ski the short distance to where the hill really begins. Then I watch him rip off down the hill. I smile wisely, and proceed slowly, but safely down to the bottom where he is waiting."

Another example:"I will never forget the time that I took 25 deaf children and their college-aged counselors on an overnight hike in a rugged wilderness area near Bozeman. We had packed enough food for dinner that night, and breakfast the next morning before we would hike back down to where we had parked the vans and cars that would take us back to our "base" camp about 3 miles away. We thought that we had included **everything** that would be needed for such an adventure: warm clothes, a sleeping bag for each camper, and everyone had his/her own flashlight. The hike was 4 1/2 miles to the top. We reached the camp site in about 2 hours. It was situated in an awesome high glacial valley of the Rocky Mountain chain. Wildflowers were "ablaze" everywhere and the creeks and nearby lake were "ice" cold from the melting snow that still "capped" the surrounding peaks. Just as we got settled and I had started a fire to cook our hotdogs for dinner, some dark clouds appeared on the horizon. Within 20 minutes it was pouring down rain! The fire went out. Everyone just stood around shivering and stamping feet to keep warm, not knowing what to say or do. Soon it was dark and too late and dangerous to start the slippery hike back down to the cars. I gathered everyone together and said, "I am very sorry for what has happened. We had no idea that it would rain up here in the middle of such a beautiful summer day! Try to get some sleep now. Maybe the bags will keep you dry." Of course, everyone was as wet and cold *inside* the bags as outside. The next morning it was a pitiful sight—the sleeping bags with steam slowly rising from them as a few hardy individuals stood around stamping their feet and rubbing their hands to keep warm. I hardly dared to make eye contact with the counselors or the children. I felt terrible! How could I have made such a stupid mistake? Never again would I take a group hiking without a plastic rain tarp big enough to cover everybody! There was a happy ending, however. After a quick, cold, wet breakfast we all started down the trail. Soon the sun came out. We all got to the bottom OK, loaded into the vehicles, and drove back to our base camp. Everyone slept that entire day. Every available clothesline, tree stump, or protruding branch had either wet clothes or sleeping bags attached. No one got sick and we all still enjoy reminiscing about our most horrible night of the year!"

Exercise #3: Dialogues

1.The student should create a "dialogue" between two or three people for class presentation for the purpose of practicing Visual Spatial Communication (VSC) concepts and ASL "colorings."

Work on: a. setting up positions of people
                b. eye contact
                c. facial expression
                d. any ASL principles (colorings), including the use of "classifiers"

For example: Teacher: Is this your first visit to Washington, D.C.?

             Student: Yes, and it has been quite an adventure for me. I have seen some of the most amazing things.

             Teacher: You mean tourist things or cultural things?

             Student: Both. My friend and I went to all the usual places like the Smithsonian and quite a few museums. But then we decided to walk to Georgetown and got lost on the way.

             Teacher: How lost?

             Student: I am embarrassed to say **very** lost! We got so turned around that we were going in the wrong direction.

             Teacher: So what happened?

             Student: My friend told me that maybe we should call a taxi. The only thing was that there was no phone and we were both afraid to go into a store to use one.

             Teacher: That does not make sense!

Student: Yes it does! Most of the stores had lots of people standing around by the door and they seemed too friendly!

Teacher: Are you trying to tell me that you had gotten off the beaten track enough to get into the wrong section of town?

Student: I'm afraid so. After two cars stopped and asked if we wanted a ride, and after we were stopped by a man selling dope, we decided to reverse our direction and head back toward the Smithsonian.

Teacher: Did you ever make it to Georgetown?

Student: Yes, but we rode the bus.

The above exercise can be signed by two people or by one person who takes on both characters.

2. Write additional dialogues. Present to your classmates.

NOTE: Students are directed to a very excellent series of stories on video cassette by SIGN A VISION, PO Box 30580, Seattle, Wa 98103-0580 (206) 789-3434 (TDD/V). They are presented in "Englished" ASL and voiced for those who are not familiar with signing.

"The Greedy Cat"
"The Magic Pot"
"The House That Jack Built"
"Village Stew"
"The Father, the Son, and the Donkey"

These stories are told by master children's storyteller, Billy Seago, a young deaf adult with extensive experience in capturing young audiences with his acting and storytelling abilities. As you watch these intriguing stories interpreted by Mr. Seago, be sure to observe the synchronization of "mouth" and "sign" and also the many ASL "colorings" that he adds for extra information. (The same stories are also available in "modern" American Sign Language.)

Exercise #4: Poetry

Select a poem, analyze it and translate it. Use free poetic license. Present the poem to the class and encourage the class to critique your efforts. This can also be accomplished as a "group" effort. Here are examples for review.

HAIKU POETRY

An old silent pond...
Into the pond
A frog jumps,
Splash! Silence again

—Basho

Snow whispering down
All day long,
Earth has vanished
Leaving only sky

—Jose

Since my house
Burned down, I now own
A better view
Of the Rising moon

—Masahide

One lone pine tree
growing in the hollow—
and I thought
I was the only one
without a friend

—Joso

The waves of the great sea,
rending, toppling,
splitting, scattering,
thunder in
upon the rocky shore

—Minamoto No Sanetomo

Where the bright moon comes up,
the sky has cleared,
through drifting clouds
linger far off
by the rim of the mountain

—Kyogoku Tamekane

So few rays
of morning sun
filter through the branches
how cool it is
deep within the bamboo!

—Kyogoku Tamekane

In the snow piled
on the bedroom roof
the hail makes no sound,
but as it slants down,
it raps at the window

—Kyogoku Tamekane

On Reading Poems to a Senior Class at South High

Before
I opened my mouth
I noticed them sitting there
as orderly as frozen fish
in a package.

Slowly water began to fill the room
though I did not notice it
till it reached
my ears

and then I heard the sounds
of fish in an aquarium

and I knew that though I had
tried to drown them
with my words

that they had only opened up
like gills for them
and let me in.

Together we swam around the room
like thirty tails whacking words
till the bell rang
puncturing
a hole in the door
where we all leaked out

They went to another class
I suppose and I home
where Queen Elizabeth
my cat met me
and licked my fins
till they were hands again.

—D.C. Berry

Richard Cory

Whenever Richard Cory went down town,
We people on the pavement looked at him:
He was a gentleman from sole to crown,
Clean favored, and imperially slim.

And he was always quietly arrayed,
And he was always human when he talked;
But still he fluttered pulses when he said,
"Good-morning," and he glittered when he walked.

And he was rich—yes, richer than a king—
And admirably schooled in every grace:
In fine, we thought that he was everything
To make us wish that we were in his place.

So on we worked and waited for the light,
And went without the meat, and cursed the bread;
And Richard Cory, one calm summer night,
Went home and put a bullet through his head.

—Edwin Arlington Robinson

The Road Not Taken

Two roads diverged in a yellow wood,
And sorry I could not travel both
And be one traveler, long I stood
And looked down one as far as I could
To where it bent in the undergrowth;

Then took the other, as just as fair,
And having perhaps the better claim,
Because it was grassy and wanted wear;
Though as for that, the passing there
Had worn them really about the same,

And both that morning equally lay
In leaves no step had trodden black.
Oh, I kept the first for another day!
Yet knowing how way leads on to way,
I doubted if I should ever come back.

I shall be telling this with a sigh
Somewhere ages and ages hence:
Two roads diverged in a wood, and I—
I took the one less traveled by,
And that has made all the difference.

—Robert Frost

The Light is Sweet

Truly the light is sweet,
And a pleasant thing it is
For the eyes to behold the sun.

The Bible

A Poison Tree

I was angry with my friend:
I told my wrath, my wrath did end.
I was angry with my foe:
I told it not, my wrath did grow.

And I watered it in fears,
Night and morning with my tears;
And I sunned it with smiles,
And with soft deceitful wiles.

And it grew both day and night
Till it bore an apple bright;
And my foe beheld it shine,
And he knew that it was mine,

And into my garden stole
When the night had veiled the pole:
In the morning glad I see
My foe outstretched beneath the tree.

—William Blake

Hold Fast Your Dreams

Hold fast your dreams!
Within your heart
Keep one still, secret spot
Where dreams may go,
And sheltered so,
May thrive and grow—
Where doubt and fear are not.
Oh, keep a place apart
Within your heart,
For little dreams to go.

—Louise Driscoll

Give Me the Splendid Silent Sun

Give me the splendid silent sun with all its beams full-dazzling,
Give me juicy autumnal fruit ripe and red from the orchard,
Give me a field where the unmowed grass grows,
Give me an arbor, give me the trellised grape,
Give me fresh corn and wheat, give me serene-moving animals teaching content.
Give me nights perfectly quiet as on high plateaus west of the Mississippi, and I am looking up at the stars
Give me ordurous at sunrise a garden of beautiful flowers where I can walk undisturbed.

—Walt Whitman

Lenox Avenue Mural/Harlem

What happens to a dream deferred?

Does it dry up
like a raisin the sun?
Or fester like a sore—
And then run?
Does it stink like rotten meat?
Or crust and sugar over—
like a syrupy sweet?
Maybe it just sags
like a heavy load.
Or does it explode?

—Langston Hughes

Beauty

Beauty is seen
In the sunlight,
The trees, the birds,
Corn growing and people working
Or dancing for their harvest.

Beauty is heard
In the night,
Wind sighing, rain falling,
Or a singer chanting
Anything in earnest.

Beauty is in yourself.
Good deeds, happy thought
That repeat themselves
In your dreams,
In your work,
And even in you rest.

—E-Yeg-Shure

O Captain! My Captain!

O Captain! my Captain! our fearful trip is done,
The ship has weathered every rack, the prize we sought is won
The port is near, the bells I hear, the people all exulting,
While follow eyes the steady keel, the vessel grim and daring;

But O heart! heart! heart!
O the bleeding drops of red,
Where on the deck my Captain lies,
Fallen cold and dead.

O Captain! my Captain! rise up and hear the bells;
Rise up—for you the flag is flung—for you the bugle trills,

For you bouquets and ribbon'd wreaths—for you the shores a-crowding
For you they call, the swaying mass, their eager faces turning;

Here, Captain! dear father!
This arm beneath your head!
It is some dream that on the deck
You've fallen cold and dead.

My Captain does not answer, his lips are pale and still,
My father does not feel my arm, he has no pulse nor will,
The ship is anchored safe and sound, its voyage closed and done,
From fearful trip the victor ship comes in with object won;

Exult, O shores! and ring, O bells!
But I, with mournful tread,
Walk the deck my Captain lies,
Fallen cold and dead.

—Walt Whitman

Exercise #5: Creating an ASL Poem

Create an ASL poem. Use only one or two handshapes. Present your poem to the class for discussion and analysis.

Here is an example using only the two handshapes "C" and "D" (or index).

See accompanying photos.
See accompanying 43 handshapes.

Culture

An ASL Poem by Bernard Bragg

Culture, deaf communication
Hearing people aside
Hearing mind aside
Listen with ears, no!
Listen with eyes, yes!
Force you? Force me? No!
You and me
Part of one culture

Elements of ASL Poetry

1. Alliteration of handshape

2. Rhyme of movement

3. Meter of sign

4. Rhythm of expression (articulation-enunciation-delivery)

5. Tone of non-manuals (emoting-inflecting)

Poetic Devices Used in ASL Poetry

1. Symbolic use of space and of directionality

2. Certain handshapes that echo the actual image (like onomatopoeic sounds)

3. Ironic contrast between facial expression and what the hands were "saying."

4. Poetic persona

43 Different Handshapes

Generally speaking, successful signers of good will send highly intelligible Visual Spatial messages by attempting to control to the best of their abilities the following four different manual components:

(1) hand location or position   (3) palm orientation
(2) hand movement or motion   (4) handshape

Improper **locationing/positioning** of the hand/s can result in a breakdown in manual communication. For example, signs that originate near the forhead usually represent "cognition" or "maleness." Signs created near the heart connote "emotion." If a signer gets off the target area for location/position, obvious problems occur because many signs share the same components except for one or two. A good example of this is what can happen when an imprecise signer attempts to make the sign for "because" but gets the movement too close to the mouth instead of the forehead. The handshape, palm orientation, and movement are the same for both "because" and "better," with just the **location** of the hand differing for the two concepts. Likewise "mother" and "father" can easily be confused as well as numerous other sign concepts.

The smooth flow of **motion** in signing also cannot be ignored. Proper motions of signs really should be learned from the trained instructor and not from a book, since it is not possible to show such variations as strength and vigor of movement and other subtleties of movement in a line drawing. For example "Come." and "Get over here right now!" are good example of how a sign can change with the **emphasis** of movement. The **motion** for the concept "teach" changes, dependent upon who is being taught — **you** or the **student**. Think about the movement for the signs "alongside," "with," "follow," "avoid," "race," "ahead," "behind," and "far." **Location** and **movement** parameters change for each of these concepts while **palm orientation** and **handshape** remain constant.

The final sign component, **handshape**, is also of utmost importance in creating clear, highly intelligible sign concepts. Be picky about this parameter of the signing process. Those individuals you are communicating with will be appreciative because of your carefulness. The amount of Visual Spatial information available to complete the communicative act will greatly increase due to your precise handshape control.

The following photographed handshapes are the 40 most basic. Remember that while 25 of these handshapes are used in INITI signs (all the letters of the manual alphabet except "z") the remaining 15 handshapes are not. Also, 25 of the basic 40 handshapes pictured can **also** be used as "classifier" shapes as well. The difference becomes clear when you contrast the basic "i" handshape for "institution," "idea," and "imagine," with the sign for "thin" that utilizes the classifier "i" handshape. The latter sign concept **takes on special meaning because of the "classifier" handshape used.** The student needs only imagine a "thin" person being represented by an imaginary thin **line** as the two "i" handshapes touch and separate.

Serious students should seek out and study all four of the sign components just described from a qualified sign instructor. The authors have conveniently listed common examples of signs under each handshape photo (basic and classifier). Additionally, three more classifier handshapes (numbers 41, 42, & 43) are listed separately as they are different from the before-mentioned 25.

Students should consider "classifiers" under the following categories: (1) size and shape of an object, (2) holding on to an instrument or object, or (3) something abstract. A good exercise would be to go through the following classifier handshapes and create a sentence for each basic shape "concept" and also for each classifier shape "concept."

BASIC SHAPE		CLASSIFER SHAPE	BASIC SHAPE		CLASSIFER SHAPE
1.	blue bachelor busy	shelf table floor	5.	empty early sick	none
2.	music please proof	book mirror window	6.	must onion apple	eagle or hawk beak hearing aid fish hook
3.	farm father fine	traffic (2 hands) prison bars (2 hands) movie (2 hands)	7.	fast run who	none
4.	drip ignore parade	stripes/plaids line of people fence	8.	exact pick on a little bit	write with pen apply lipstick apply eye shadow

BASIC SHAPE		CLASSIFER SHAPE

BASIC SHAPE		CLASSIFER SHAPE

9.   bug
     devil
     listen to

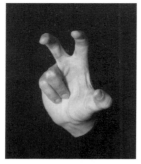

eagle's claw
pitch a ball

10.   blind
     doubt
     potato

lift
dead animal

11.   crazy
     freeze
     yell / scream

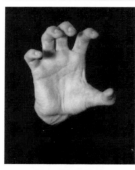

soft ball (2 hands)
door knob
basket ball (2 hands)

12.   chocolate
     class
     certificate

column
cup
tube

13.   alcoholic drink
     eye glasses
     priest

liquid (amount)
belt buckle
collar

14.   equal
     invite
     night

15.   expensive (B,A)
     altogether (A,B)
     Jewish (A,B,A,B)

camera flash (B,A,B)
shower (B,A,B,A)
suction (A,B,A,B)

16.   family
     decide
     curious

button
pipe (steel)
key hole

BASIC SHAPE		CLASSIFER SHAPE	BASIC SHAPE		CLASSIFER SHAPE
17.	west Wednesday water	none	21.	kill party purple	none

18.	see
	purpose (mean)
	stuck
		snake
		person riding on
		  animal, bike or
		  motorcyle
		2 persons "eyeing"
		  each other
			22.	diamond
				divorce
				doctor
					none

19.	rooster
	lousy
	dignify
		car or motorized
		  vehicle (including a
		  submarine)
		garage
			23.	team
				toilet
				tan
					none

20.	use egg hospital	bandaid stamp	24.	coffee exaggerate work	shift stick

BASIC SHAPE		CLASSIFER SHAPE	BASIC SHAPE		CLASSIFER SHAPE
25.	audiology aunt secret	wash a window	29.	more food or eat flower	hat napkin cloth

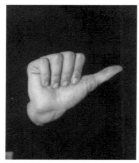

26.	yourself challenge establish	bottles (abstract) house (abstract) lamp (abstract)	30.	duck no clothespin	none

27.	east elementary evaluate	none	31.	bird green group	frame (outline) eyebrows moustache

28.	office zero organization	none	32.	hate melon terrible	none

BASIC SHAPE		CLASSIFER SHAPE	BASIC SHAPE		CLASSIFER SHAPE
33.	delicious like meat	none	37.	cow play measure	fat person (waddle) telephone horns
34.	ready religion responsible	curlers rope braids	38.	airplane I-Love-You airplane land, take off, crash, etc	airplane (abstract)
35.	idea jealous institution	thin	39.	cigarette kid whiskey	none
36.	later lazy next in line	pistol innoculation device	40.	opposite false for	toothbrush hotdogs (on grill) telephone poles (flash by)

BASIC SHAPE   **CLASSIFER SHAPE**

41. harmonica

book (thickness)
magazine (thickness)
sandwich (thickness)
VCR

42.

fishing pole
paint brush

43.

string (indicate
thinness)
tissue (indicate thinness)
paper (indicate thinness)

Practice Stories

The stories (5) in the following section are all true, as are the two stories in the main part of the book ("Crackers" and "Experiences"). They are based on the lives of the authors or news-worthy events.

Please attempt to express yourself as you proceed to go through the stories. No pictures are given, and only minimal clues are suggested. Probably the best approach is to go through the stories as a class exercise with a teacher trained in ASL; however, it is possible to sign everything word-for-word, depending upon your skill level.

THE NEWLYWEDS

Bernard Bragg

I have heard this story told many times by my parents and their friends. I think it followed my mother and father all through their lives. I have actually seen people laugh so hard that tears would come to their eyes! Now, that has to be a wonderful story! Here's how it goes:

My parents, who are both deaf, too, were married in the traditional Jewish ceremony by a rabbi under a canopy. After the wine was drunk and the glass smashed and the party finished, my folks boarded a train for Pennsylvania for their honeymoon. Arrangements had been made for them to stay at a quaint country inn that specialized in honeymoons. After checking in they went straight to bed. But this is not the end of the story! The next morning they came downstairs to the dining room and ordered their breakfast. As they sat there, basking in the glow of their love and the new life they were beginning together, they noticed that they were being carefully scrutinized by the other honeymooning guests sitting at adjoining tables. It seemed that some were even giggling and whispering along with their "eyeing." My parents of course became very uncomfortable—were these people making fun of their deafness? My father, furious, stomped into the manager's office and wrote "Why is everyone mocking us?" The manager, avoiding eye contact and red with embarrassment, wrote back "I think you'd better go up to your room and look under the bed—then you will understand." My father rushed up to the room and kneeled on the floor and lifted up the bedspread and what did he see—a shiny brass cowbell!

When my parents celebrated their 35th wedding anniversary, their friends brought a large surprise cake and the theme for the cake decoration, as you can already guess, was a miniature bed on top with a tiny bell under it. You might say that I was conceived into the world with the loud ringing of the bell that I didn't hear!

The Newlyweds
Clues for Visual - Spatial Presentation

WORDS	PRINCIPLES	DESCRIPTIONS
"laugh so hard"	ASL idiom	Claws both hands, palms in the vicinity of the stomach as if stomach were shaking
"tears would come	ASL type	repeat "tears"
to their eyes"	Be sure to lipsynch	
"has to be"	PARA "must"	lipsynch
"Here's how it goes"	PARA "proceed"	lipsynch
"traditional"	ASL type	alternatingly roll both hands off R shoulder
"Rabbi"	PICTO-like	R's down ears represents curled hair hanging down
"under a canopy"	PICTO-like	outline the canopy above
"my folks"	PARA "parents"	lipsynch
"boarded a train"	ASL type COMBO	show sign for "sitting" in a vehicle, then "train" with movement out
"Pennsylvania"	DACTO	fingerspell "PA"
"honeymoon"	ASL type	touch both sides of chin with middle finger
"quaint"	PARA "old"	lipsynch
"country inn"	DACTO	fingerspell "inn"
"after checking in"	ASL type COMBO	"signature" + "in"

WORDS	PRINCIPLES	DESCRIPTIONS
"to bed"	ASL type	indicate 4 legs going to
"they went **downstairs**"	ASL type	the index finger represents the couple, showing them coming down
"**ordered**"	PARA "command"	lipsynch
"**basking in the glow of their love**"	ASL type	flutter fingertips up chest + "love" lipsynch

(there are probably various other ways to sign these phrases according to ASL background)

"guests"	fingerspell	lipsynch
"adjoining tables"	ASL type	"near tables," "near tables" move from right to left to indicate location
"giggling"	ASL type	scratch the corners of the mouth with the indexes
"eyeing"	ASL type directional	"v's" represent the eyes of the other guests as they "eye" or "stare" at the deaf couple
"of course"	PARA "true" or ASL "naturally"	
"**u**ncomfortable"	ASL type	1) shake head to indicate negation, or 2) fingerspell "un", or 3) sign under chin
"making fun of"	PARA "mock"	directional verb toward deaf couple
"stomped"	ASL type	exaggerated "walk"

WORDS	PRINCIPLES	DESCRIPTIONS
"avoided eye contact"		can be signed literally, but ASL "color" can be added with proper facial expression and movement of the eyes
"rushed up to"	ASL type PARA "run"	indicate movement was accomplished quickly
"lifted up the bedspread"	ASL mime	
"cowbell"	COMBO	"cow" + "bell"
"anniversary"	ASL type COMBO	"yearly" + "celebration"
"theme"	COMBO	"idea" + "specific"
"cake **decoration**"	ASL type PICTO-like	fingertips of both hands touch and twist as you make a circle as if you were sprinkling something on top of the cake
"miniature"	PARA small	lipsynch
"conceived"	ASL type	intermingle fingertips of "5" handshape

THE DAY THEY CHOSE A DEAF PRESIDENT

Jack Olson

Living in Bozeman, Montana, can be a very isolating experience if you are in the field of "deafness." There are only 4 or 5 deaf people in the whole city, maybe 10 in the county, and about 500 in the entire state. Sometimes I get lucky, however, and have the chance to communicate with a deaf tourist or a deaf college student passing through, but those encounters are far and few between.

Imagine my surprise at home one evening, when my wife Val yelled at me from another room to turn on the small TV in my study. It took a few seconds for the picture to appear, but through the fuzzy black and white picture, the image of a young man appeared. He was rapidly signing something to a news commentator—an interpreter in the background gave him voice. Watching carefully, I soon learned that Gallaudet University was involved in a serious crisis. Students were angry and hostile! They were boycotting classes and demonstrating in front of the administration building. American Sign Language flew fast and furious across the TV screen! Hey, this was really exciting—too exciting to watch on a small black and white TV! I quickly ran to the living room to join Val and watched the remainder of the broadcast on the larger color set. Nothing like this had ever happened before—and on national news to boot! Deaf people demonstrating? Deaf people demanding their rights? They had mostly been known as a "silent" minority with no history of demonstration or protest. It was a new and different experience for me—watching these deaf students "speaking" out against an unjust situation in a very forceful and effective way.

All of this was made no less impressive by my isolation from Gallaudet and all that it stands for—research, a mecca for deaf culture and community, and higher education. The reasons for the protest made perfect sense to me, and I think the same message came through loud and clear to millions of other Americans that night and succeeding days and nights of very excellent news coverage.

Quite simply, the deaf community of Gallaudet University (and probably the deaf people of the entire U.S.) were tired of being patronized by the hearing! The fact that a new hearing president had been chosen, by a mostly hearing board, instead of an equally qualified deaf candidate, not only seemed unjust, but it was the straw that broke the camel's back. This time deaf students were not going to take it sitting down. By boycotting classes they effectively shut down the **entire** university! They refused to believe or trust a new hearing president who did not know sign language or anything about their community and culture. They were not the least bit convinced when the newly appointed leader promised to learn their sign language at her earliest convenience and also study their special needs.

I found myself tingling with pride and excitement as I watched the deaf students take care of the situation in their own way—peacefully, but forcefully, they protested, and silently, but courageously, they did not give up! In the end, the newly selected president resigned and went back to her old job. In her place, a deaf man named I. King Jordon was appointed. For the first time in 124 years, Gallaudet University has a President who is creating a new image of deaf people in the eyes of the world.

The Day They Chose a Deaf President

Clues for Visual - Spatial Presentation

WORDS	PRINCIPLES	DESCRIPTIONS
"isolating"	INITI or PARA "alone"	lipsynch
"field"	INITI or PARA "major"	lipsynch
"county"	fingerspell	
"get"	PARA "become"	lipsynch
"chance"	INITI, or PARA "opportunity"	lipsynch "
"tourist"	use "tour" or "trip"	plus "person" sign
"**passing** through"	use formal sign for "pass"	plus "through"
"encounters"	PARA "meets"	lipsynch
"another **room**"	ASL type	lipsynch
"study"	COMBO	"study" + "room"
"picture **to** appear"	PICTO-like	imagine the picture coming on, fist to open "5"
"**fuzzy** black and white picture"	PARA "vague"	lipsynch
"**i**mage"	INITI, or PARA "picture"	lipsynch "

WORDS	PRINCIPLES	DESCRIPTIONS
"commentator"	PARA "speaker"	lipsynch
"**b**ackground"	INITI	lipsynch
"crisis"	PARA "conflict" or COMBO	"difficult" + "trouble"
"hostile"	PARA "unfriendly"	"friend" + "negation" sign
"boycotting"	PARA "leave" or fingerspell	
"**d**emonstrating"	INITI, or PARA "show"	lipsynch "
"**adm**inistration"	fingerspell "adm"	loan sign
"flew fast and furious"	ASL idiom	alternate opening and closing fists as you move first one hand and then the other outward from the chest, lipsynch
"**remainder** of the"	ASL type	place hands in front of the chest, palms in, RH behind LH, they touch then the RH moves out
"broadcast"	PARA "information" COMBO	"information" + "exaggerate" movement
"news"	PARA "information"	spreading motion, flat "O's" to open "5's" from forehead
"to boot"	PARA "plus" or "add"	put this sign **after** "before" in the sentence
"silent **minority**"	fingerspell	

WORDS	PRINCIPLES	DESCRIPTIONS
"protest"	PARA "disobey"	fists touch forehead (knuckles) and then sharply twist out
"speaking out against"	ASL type	fists on chest open to "5's", palms up (as if you are getting it off your chest) or sign it literally lipsynch
"made perfect **sense**"	PARA "mind"	lipsynch
"message"	PARA "information"	lipsynch
"**succeeding** days and nights"	ASL type	repeat "next" several times, lipsynch
"news **coverage**"	ASL type	LH fist, RH open "5" sweeps over the LH and circles once
"**quite** simply"	PARA "very"	lipsynch
"patronized"	PARA "pity"	lipsynch
"hearing"	ASL type	(index circular on chin)
"the **fact**"	PARA "proof"	lipsynch
"equally **q**ualified"	INITI	circle "q" to heart
"candidate"	PARA "applicant"	lipsynch
"straw that broke the camel's back"	sign this literally	lipsynch
"were **not going to**	(will not) PARA "refuse"	lipsynch

WORDS	PRINCIPLES	DESCRIPTIONS
take it sitting down"	(accept)	facial expression
"effectively shut down"	PARA "successfully" + "stopped"	lipsynch
"entire"	PARA "all"	lipsynch
"least bit"	ASL type	grasp the little finger of the RH with the thumb and forefinger of the LH and flick the thumb off the little finger
"earliest **convenience**"	PARA "comfort"	lipsynch
"**tingle** with pride"	ASL type	flutter "5" hands, palms in, up chest, use standard signs for "with" and "pride"
"give up"	PARA "surrender"	lipsynch
"resigned"	PARA "quit"	lipsynch
"in her place"	PARA "exchange"	lipsynch
"appointed"	PARA "select"	lipsynch
"**i**mage"	INITI	"i" to the palm of the hand

THE DAY I ALMOST GOT FIRED FOR SIGNING

Jack Olson

When I first started teaching the deaf, I though that I had the perfect job. I taught math and reading to a class of 5th graders every day. The rest of the time I worked with the entire intermediate department of about 75 deaf children, trying to improve their oral communication skills. Soon I had them all involved in a musical play that they had written themselves. There were a number of Mitch Miller songs that they "sang" as well as lines that they were required to speak. The school where I taught was supposed to be oral and the administration was very proud that they gave every deaf child the opportunity to learn to speak early on in their education. Most of the children in my speech classes were into their early teens and not many could speak well. As we rehearsed for our play, it soon became obvious to me that it was going to be impossible for me to direct the students on the stage without using at least a few signs! My supervising teacher was horrified! She reminded me that our school was oral and that it would **not** be good for public relations if I were seen signing to the students in the presence of a mixed deaf/hearing audience. She told me to continue to do the best that I could with speech reading. Well, I tried, but I knew that her suggestions would **not** work. I felt sorry for the students who needed a more dependable way to follow the music on the stage. So I secretly continued to use speech with signs and fingerspelling for better understanding with my classroom door closed.

One day the assistant director of the teacher training program brought some teacher trainees to my room to observe me teaching speech. I thought it would be a good idea to show them some of the songs that we were preparing for the show. The students, eager to please, put on their headsets and I turned on the music. We all commenced "singing" our favorite Mitch Miller song "Down in the Valley." Unfortunately, I forgot to **not** use my clue signs. The angry assistant director went directly to the superintendent's office afterwards and demanded that I be fired for embarrassing her in front of her students! The superintendent smiled and reminded her that I was doing a fine job with the students and that sometimes it was OK to be a little bit flexible. It did not take long for the story to get back to me about what had really happened. I was thankful that my boss had supported me and was broadminded enough back in 1963 to realize that a few signs would not hurt my attempts to make my students feel more secure and comfortable in their first live theater attempt.

Later, when we did the show before a large appreciative audience of both deaf and hearing people, I did another very sneaky thing. The theme for the production was "Hawaii," and I got the idea of building myself a grass hut, stage left, and hiding myself in the hut so only the children on stage could see me. That way I could keep them in time with my signs and no one in the audience ever knew what I was doing. Since then, attitudes toward sign language have changed so very much. If I had to do it all over again today, I'd have my students "sing" the songs in their own visual language, with one or two hearing singers to accompany them "a la" NTD style.

The Day I Almost Got Fired for Signing

Clues for Visual - Spatial Communication

WORDS	PRINCIPLES	DESCRIPTIONS
"job"	PARA "work"	lipsynch
"graders"	fingerspell	
"intermediate"	ASL type	same handshapes as for "between," double movement
"**d**epartment"	INITI collective noun	lipsynch
"**adm**inistration"	fingerspell "adm"	loan sign
"into"	ASL "enter"	lipsynch
"early teens" fingerspell "teens"	PARA "young"	lipsynch
"**r**ehearsed"	PARA "practice" INITI	lipsynch
"obvious"	PARA "clear"	lipsynch
"**d**irect"	PARA "control" INITI	use "x's", lipsynch
"at least"	fingerspell	lipsynch
"**supervising** teacher"	PARA "care"	cross "k" hands, slow counterclockwise circle in front of chest
"reminded"	use same sign for "remember"	

WORDS	PRINCIPLES	DESCRIPTIONS
"**p**ublic **r**elations"	INITI	lipsynch
"her suggestions would not **work**"	PARA "success"	lipsynch
"eager"	PARA "enthusiasm"	lipsynch
"put on their headsets"	ASL mime	lipsynch
"**turned on** the music"	ASL mime	lipsynch
"unfortunately"	fingerspell "un" + PARA "lucky"	lipsynch
"**clue** signs"	fingerspell	lipsynch
"went **directly to**"	ASL type	indicate movement, indexes pointing out, move from chest outward
"to get **back to me**"	ASL type	RH palm out, index up circles out then in toward self
"attempts"	PARA "try"	lipsynch
"we **did the show**"	PARA "finish"	lipsynch
"sneaky"	PARA "hide"	lipsynch
"theme"	COMBO "specific" + "idea"	lipsynch
"keep them in time with my signs"	use regular signs, but do so rhythmically	

WORDS	PRINCIPLES	DESCRIPTIONS
"ever"	fingerspell	lipsynch
"since then"	ASL type	exaggerated "since," lipsynch
" all **over** again"	fingerspell	lipsynch
"**v**isual language"	INITI	"v" from corner of eye, move out, palm out
"accompany"	PARA "follow"	lipsynch
"a la NTD"	fingerspell or PARA "way"	lipsynch

THE THREE WHALES WHO GOT STUCK IN THE ICE

Jack Olson

Let me tell you the true story about the three leviathans who got stuck in the ice! Maybe you remember seeing their pictures in the newspaper or evening news during the last two weeks of October, 1988, fighting for their lives in the rapidly freezing ocean north of the Arctic Circle, and not far from Barrow, Alaska. If you bother to look at a map, you'll agree that you can't get much further north than Barrow, Alaska! At any rate, the whales should have left the area about two weeks earlier and they were in serious trouble, swimming around in circles below the ice, struggling to find air in the ever narrowing airhole. The hole was so small that the three had to take turns to come up, often hitting the sharp edges of the hole with their heads, cutting themselves in the process. When the Eskimos first found them they did **not** do what they usually do when they find whales in such a predicament. Probably they reacted in this kindly manner because the news media discovered the whales about the same time and it wasn't long before the whole world got caught up in the drama. It seemed that just about everybody became involved in trying to save those whales! First the Eskimos attempted to chip the breathing hole larger, but it did not help much because of the intense cold. Then, two young men from Minnesota flew up there and brought a special machine they had invented that helped widen the breathing hole considerably. Soon the Eskimos thought of using chainsaws and really made a big hole. It was not long before they discovered that they could move the whales toward the open sea by cutting successive holes about 250 feet apart and then encouraging them to move under the ice to each new hole. However, it was a slow process and over four and one half miles stood between them and the open channel. Another obstacle, a thick ice ridge, also blocked their way. From the pictures I saw on TV, it looked like an almost impossible task. I really started to feel sorry for those battered animals! To make matters worse, one of them died and sank out of sight and I was sure that the other two would soon suffer a similar fate! It was truly heart rending to see them push up for air every few seconds before sinking back beneath the cold surface of the water. Fortunately, the saga of the three whales stuck in the ice ended happily when the Russian government, with permission from the U.S., brought in a huge icebreaker and smashed a wide channel through the thick ice ridge to free the remaining trapped whales. All of this effort cost more than $800,000. Some say, among other things, that it wasn't worth it and that animals don't have rights and that we have no business directing our sentimental attentions on saving animals when there are so many **people** in trouble everywhere! But, I disagree. As far as I am concerned, anytime the world can be tuned in and made to react with sensitivity and concern for any animal, no matter how big or small, important or unimportant, we all gain from that experience; and the world becomes a better place in which to live!

The Three Whales Who Got Stuck in the Ice

Clues for Visual - Spatial Communication

WORDS	PRINCIPLES	DESCRIPTIONS
"got"	PARA "became"	lipsynch
"stuck"	ASL type	"v" handshape, move quickly to the neck
"evening **news**"	PARA "information"	lipsynch
"Arctic Circle"	fingerspell "Arctic" standard sign for "Circle"	lipsynch
"map"	fingerspell	lipsynch
"At any rate"	ASL type PARA "never-the-less"	lipsynch
"**a**rea"	PARA "place" INITI	lipsynch
"swimming around in		This phrase is an excellent opportunity to practice PICTO-like signing: "circles below the ice." Think of the whales swimming in circles (use your RH) under the ice (use your left arm horizontally positioned in front of the chest, palm down to represent the ice sheet). The entire phrase could be signed with just those two hand positions plus lipsynchronization of the phrase.
"ever"	PARA "always"	lipsynch

WORDS	PRINCIPLES	DESCRIPTIONS
"narrowing"	PICTO-like	indicate successive narrowings of the hole by bringing the "c" handshapes successively inward—for example, the hole starts out big, then gets smaller, lipsynch
"airhole"	PICTO-like	trace the outline of the airhole with index, lift eyes upward as if you were under the water looking up
"take turns to come up"	PICTO-like	Use both hands to represent the whales, alternating as they come up for air. Be imaginative! As the animals burst through the water, the fists could open up to indicate the splashing of the water and the instant condensation of the warm air coming from their blowholes. ASL involvement of the mouth could also indicate the animals' struggle to breathe by puffing out the cheeks and exploding air.
"predicament"	PARA "situation"	lipsynch
"**reacted**"	INITI	"r's" from the mouth palms out, lipsynch
"it wasn't long"	PARA "soon"	lipsynch
"media"	fingerspell	lipsynch
"got caught up"	PARA "fascinated"	lipsynch
"**save**"	PARA "**free**" or INITI	lipsynch
"chip the breathing holes **larger**"	ASL PICTO-like	mime "chopping", then show shape of hole both hands, hole widens

WORDS	PRINCIPLES	DESCRIPTIONS
"considerably"	PARA "much"	lipsynch
"chainsaws"	ASL PICTO	imagine holding a chainsaw and moving it up and down making a buzzing sound with your mouth
"cutting successive holes"	ASL PICTO-like	use your chainsaw, then indicate successive holes with indexes outlining them all the while moving from the R to L, lipsynch
"to move under the ice"	ASL PICTO-like	place left arm horizontally to indicate ice, then RH "B" shape moves up and down, R to L as if whales move from one hole to next
"obstacle"	PARA "stop"	lipsynch
"ice ridge"	PICTO-like	indicate the ridge with a movement of the right hand to outline the ridge, lipsynch
"impossible"	ASL type	"y" handshape taps the left palm, double movement with negative head shake, lipsynch
"task"	PARA "work"	lipsynch
"battered"	PARA "hurt"	lipsynch
"to make **matters** worse"	PARA "things"	lipsynch
"sank out of sight"	ASL PICTO-like	the R hand slowly moves down, to show the whale's descent to the ocean floor
"similar **fate**"	PARA "death"	lipsynch
"push up for air"	ASL PICTO-like	alternate with hands flat "b" shape representing the whales as they come up for air, lipsynch

WORDS	PRINCIPLES	DESCRIPTIONS
"sinking back beneath"	ASL PICTO-like	keep LH horizontal to indicate water surface, RH move slowly down, lipsynch
"surface of the water"	ASL PICTO-like	indicate the water's surface with both hands palms down, flutter fingertips, move apart, lipsynch
"fortunately"	PARA "lucky"	lipsynch
"saga"	PARA "story"	lipsynch
"**p**ermission"	PARA "allow" INITI	lipsynch
"icebreaker"	PICTO-like action PARA "boat"	indicate forward movement of the the ship as it batters the ice, lipsynch
"smashed"	PICTO-like	strike/slice fists, lipsynch
"remaining"	PARA "last"	lipsynch
"trapped"	PARA "stuck"	lipsynch
"effort"	PARA "trying" or "work"	lipsynch
"**w**orth"	PARA "important" INITI	lipsynch
"sentimental"	PARA "pity"	lipsynch
"world **tuned in**"	PARA "contact"	lipsynch
"sensitivity"	ASL type	create the sign for "feel" with dominant hand, downward,outward, flick, lipsynch
"gain"	PARA "profit"	lipsynch

THE BEEFEATER CATASTROPHE
(In a three-way conversation)

Bernard Bragg

Cast of characters: Bernard Bragg - himself
Tom Posedly - a deaf architect
Penny Posedly - Tom's wife (hearing)

Several years ago I visited my friends, the Possedlys, who reside in Tucson, Arizona. One evening we went to a posh restaurant situated on a nearby mountain top. The view of the city lights below was spectacular! A tall, young waiter came to our table and asked us if we would like something from the bar. Penny offered to order for me, but I said, "No, I will speak for myself." Clearing my throat, I turned to the waiter and spoke my order as best as I knew. The waiter nodded his head and rapidly wrote the order on his pad. Now it was Tom's turn to order, but he "signed" his order to Penny who interpreted for him orally. After the waiter left, Penny smiled at me and said, "Oh, Bernard, I never knew you could speak!" "Why not?" I signed cockily. "To think of all the years I spent trying to learn to speak!" She said, "How admirable! My husband just refuses to speak, although he can if he wants to." I replied, "Well, to each his own." Soon the waiter came and placed the drinks on the table. My eyes widened when I saw my drink. It was in a very tall glass and was orangish-pink in color with a slice of lime and a cherry stuck on the top. I must have looked horrified because the waiter asked, "What's wrong?" "Is this mine?" I gestured. The waiter replied, "Yes, isn't that what you ordered?" I shook my head negatively. "Oh, I am sorry, what did you order?" I asked Penny to please ask him what **he thought** I said. "Oh, I don't think I can interpret that or even fingerspell it!" Puzzled, the waiter asked Penny what I really wanted for my drink. I signed to Penny, "Beefeater martini up with a lemon twist." "Wow, I am sorry I did not hear you right," said the waiter. I looked at him, smiled and spoke, "I am afraid you did not!" "That's all right, I'll get you your martini." He took away the drink that I had "invented" but did not dare to drink. Penny patted my hand sympathetically. "That's OK, Bernard. You need not feel badly. You speak much better than my husband." I shrugged my shoulders and said, "Probably so, but Tom is much smarter. He kept his mouth shut!"

The Beefeater Catastrophe
Clues for Visual - Spatial Communication

WORDS	PRINCIPLES	DESCRIPTIONS
"reside"	PARA "live"	lipsynch
"posh"	PARA "fancy"	lipsynch
"situated"	PARA "established"	lipsynch
"Tucson"	INITI	Tucson = "t" drawn like a "7,"
"Arizona"	INITI	Arizona = "a" touch one side of the chin and then the other

(Note: major cities and all states have their own sign)

WORDS	PRINCIPLES	DESCRIPTIONS
"city lights below"	ASL PICTO-like	lipsynch sign **city** as a standard sign, then **lights**, then indicate lights are sparkling by fluttering the fingertips, palms down in small circles; **below** is understood
"spectacular"	PARA "wonderful"	lipsynch
"bar"	ASL type	"a" handshape, thumb brought toward mouth, lipsynch
"offered"	PARA "give"	lypsynch ASL directional
"to order"	PARA "ask"	lipsynch
"clearing my throat"	mime sign	RH on throat
"turned to"	ASL type	natural turn of the head, direction of eyes, lipsynch or use "v" shape RH with appropriate movement

WORDS	PRINCIPLES	DESCRIPTIONS
"pad"	PICTO	mime turning the pages (bottom to top) lipsynch
"Tom's turn"	ASL type	"L" handshape RH, palm down, palm up lipsynch
"after"	ASL type "finish"	lipsynch
"cockily"	ASL type PARA for "big head"	modified "c" handshape both hands, touch temples, then move out to the side, lipsynch
"all the years"	ASL type	repeat the sign for "years," lipsynch
"spent"	PARA "continued"	lipsynch
"admirable"	PARA "wonderful"	lipsynch
"just"	fingerspell or PARA "always"	lipsynch
"if"	fingerspell	lipsynch
"well"	fingerspell	lipsynch
"his"	ASL type	repeat movement 2-3 times, palm out, move to right, lipsynch
"placed the drinks on the table"	ASL type	mime placing drinks on the tables, you can include the formal sign for "table," lipsynch
"eyes widened"	ASL type	"c's" corner of eyes, open up, lipsynch
"tall glass"	ASL type	mime sticking the cherry on the top, lipsynch
"looked horrified"	PARA "shocked"	lipsynch with appropriate facial expression

WORDS	PRINCIPLES	DESCRIPTIONS
"shook my head"	ASL	mime, plus lipsynch
"opened his pad"	ASL	mime, plus lipsynch
"startled"	PARA "surprised"	lipsynch
"even"	fingerspell	lipsynch
"Beefeater martini, up, with a lemon twist"	fingerspell the name of	lipsynch the entire phrase as you fingerspell the entire drink, regular signs for "with a lemon" use natural gesture, for "twist" use "f's"
"right"	PARA "correct"	lipsynch
"looked at him"	ASL type	you have a choice—sign this phrase literally or sign "look" and direct the sign up toward the "positioned" waiter, lipsynch
"took away the drink"	ASL mime	lipsynch
"**d**are"	fingerspell or "d" from heart outward INITI	lipsynch
"patted my hand"	ASL mime	lipsynch
"sympathetically"	PARA "pity"	lipsynch
"shrugged my shoulders"	ASL mime	lipsynch
"mouth shut"	ASL type	"b" handshapes, palms in facing mouth, move them as closing a window, lipsynch

Additional Signs to Consider

The following list of signs represents the authors' attempt to expand the receptive/expressive sign pool. This list is based on the 1,000 most commonly used word list (Voelker, 1942). All of the signs have been created according to the 5 categories (COMBO-SIGN, PARA-SIGN, PICTO-SIGN, DACTO-SIGN, and INTI-SIGN). Regional differences need to be taken into account. This list should make an interesting and challenging project for students to undertake as a group project. Consult your teacher or native Deaf signer as needed. See Sternberg (1981) for extensive treatment of sign synonyms throughout the dictionary.

DACTO sign plus lipsynch

a . . . . fingerspell
an . . . . fingerspell
back**g**round . . . . ("bg" against palm)
bit . . . . or sign "a little bit"
but . . . . (fingerspelled loan sign) also can be signed
did . . . . (fingerspelled loan sign)
do . . . . (used in ASL idiom "do, do")
does . . . . (if necessary)
due . . . . (as in "due to the fact")
if . . . . also can be signed
isn't . . . . spell "is", sign "n't"
it . . . . fingerspell
its . . . . fingerspell or can also use "possessive pro-noun handshape," (flat "b" handshape, palm out), e.g. Its tail is broken.
he . . . . fingerspell or point
her . . . . can also use "possessive pronoun handshape" e.g. Her car is nice.
his . . . . can also use "possessive pronoun handshape" e.g. His bike is blue.
him . . . . fingerspell or point
I'm . . . . fingerspell or sign "me"
of . . . . fingerspell
off . . . . fingerspell
opportunity . . . . "op"

out . . . . fingerspell or use sign
own . . . . as in "I own my house,"can be signed "have"
she . . . . fingerspell or point
so . . . . fingerspell
the . . . . fingerspell
thus . . . . fingerspell
up . . . . fingerspell or sign "to get up in the morning" or "upstairs;" this word is in a lot of phrases
vips . . . . fingerspell
7 up . . . . fingerspell

PARA sign plus lipsynch

accomplish . . . . . (as in "succeed")
according . . . . . . "follow" (as in "according to these principles")
take **advantage** of (ASL type, feel finger on palm, pull out) the advantage of buying a Chrysler instead of a Ford. "positive"
amendment . . . . . (as in "add")
amount . . . . (as in "sum" or "total")
apparent . . . . (as in "clearly," "obviously," "evidently")
apparently . . . . . . (as in "seems") Apparently you are leaving now.
apply . . . . (as in "volunteer" or "file")
article . . . . (as in "chapter") the newspaper article; (as in article of clothing) fingerspell

bonuses . . . . COMBO "money" +"present"

chief . . . . (as in "important" or "main")

company . . . . (as in "group") or fingerspell "co" (as in "going to have company tonight") sign "visitors"

composed . . . . . . (as in "calm" or "tranquil") or (as in "composed of") sign "made"

concerned . . . . . (as in "worried") or (as in "sympathy") ASL type, use "feel" handshape, alternate on/off chest

condition . . . . . . (as in "sickness") Her condition was critical; (as in "economic condition" of the country) fingerspell

consideration . . . (as in "thinking") use both hands

debt . . . . (as in "owe")

define . . . . (as in "describe" or "explain") or fingerspell

definite . . . . (as in "exact" using "f" handshape)

design . . . . (as in "art")

direct . . . . (as in "point") or (as in "direct" communication) use flat handshape, outward point

disadvantage . . . (as in "minus")

drastic . . . . (as in "terrible") He took drastic measures

duty . . . . (as in "job" or "work")

effect . . . . (as in "influence") The effect of the storm was devastating.

efficient . . . . (as in "smooth") He was an efficient worker.

element . . . . (as in "weather") It's guaranteed against the elements; (as in "some") There is the element of fear; (as in "stove element") mime or fingerspell

elementary . . . . . (as in "easy" or "simple") These tasks are elementary.

else . . . . (as in "other") Who else wants to go?

entire . . . . (as in "full" or "complete" or "all") The entire room reeked.

evident . . . . (as in "clear") His guilt was evident.

evidence . . . . (as in "prove") The evidence was circumstantial.

examination . . . . (as in "search") Examination of the room was complete; (ASL type, index off nose, double movement on palm; (as in "evaluation") The examination was very difficult.

exist . . . . (as in "address" or "live") He is barely existing or he is allowed to exist, or fingerspell

experiment . . . . . (as in "science") The experiment was successful.

extent . . . . (as in "serious" or "limit") What is the extent of his illness?

fair . . . . (as in "even") To play fair; (as in "white") Her skin is very fair; (as in "pretty") Who is the fairest of them all?

familiar . . . . (use the sign for "know") Her name seems familiar.

financial . . . . (as in "fund") We need to make financial arrangements.

form . . . . (as in "make") Form a ball with the clay; (as in "get the form for me") outline a box, ASL type

front . . . . (as in "fake") The store was a front for drug dealers.

fundamental . . . . (as in "basic") The fundamental purpose

furnish . . . . (as in "decorate" or ASL "put" "put") Furnish a house; (as in "give") Furnish me with proof

game . . . . (as in "willing") I am game if you are; (as in "animal") Wild game tastes delicious

generation . . . . . . (as in "heritage") ASL type, alternatively roll "g's" off shoulder

great . . . . (as in "wonderful," "marvelous," "fantastic," or "fabulous") I had a great time last night.

however . . . . (as in "doesn't matter" or "but") The words seem easy, however, don't be misled.

imply . . . . (as in "mean") What did she imply by those words?

income . . . . (as in "earn") My income is the same as last year.

instrument ..... (as in "tool") a dentist's instrument, fingerspell; (as in "helpful") He was instrumental in her recovery; (as in "way") He used it as an instrument for peace

just .... (as in "merely," "only," or "simply") He is just a boy; (as in "recently") I just saw her; (as in "judge") He was a just man; (as in "exact") Do it just like me.

maintain .... (as in "continue") Maintain your composure; (as in "care taker") Maintain your house.

major .... (as in "specialize") What is your major?

manner or means (as in "way") She does it in a certain manner, or It is only a means to an end

manufacture .... (as in "make") They manufacture toys.

mite .... (as in "a little bit") He's a mite slow.

modern .... (as in "new" or "now") The house is very modern.

nearly......... (as in "almost," "narrowly," "scarcely," or "barely") She nearly died.

object .... (as in "goal" or "focus") The object of my affection; (as in "thing") Put the object on the table.

occasion....... (as in "time") It was a happy occasion; (as in "event") It was a big occasion, ASL type, feel fingers to chest, then exaggerated movement upward

occur .... (as in "happen," "result," or "chance") It occurred late at night.

order .... (as in "requested") He ordered dinner early. (as in "command") He ordered her to leave.

ordinary .... (as in "natural" or "common") It was no ordinary occasion.

particular ...... (as in "specific") Select a particular car; (as in "fussy" or "complain") Don't be so particular.

personal........ (as in "secret" or "private") It's personal business.

phase .... (as in "time era" or "process") He's into the "terrible twos" phase.

physics......... (as in "electric") Physics is hard.

piece........... (as in ASL "part" or "some") Give me a piece of the cake.

position .... (as in "place") It's in the correct position; (as in "put") Position the chair closer to the sofa

practical........ (as in "common" or "standard") Be more practical.

quality .... (as in "good") This is a quality paint job.

quite........... (as in "very") She was quite pretty.

require .... (as in "demand") He requires a blood transfusion.

reserve .... (as in "save" or "enage") Reserve that room for me; (as in "cache") Use sign for "save," also A reserve of food, His cache was secure in the tree; (as in "dignified") He was a very reserved person, or fingerspell

reversible ...... (as in "change") The coat was reversible.

scarce .... (as in "gone") ASL type, It's scarce.

sense .... (as in "feel") She has a sense for creativity.

society .... (as in "class") He became a member of society when he won the money.

tangible .... (as in "touchable") The tangible results of sunshine, ASL type, open and close "8" hand configuration repeatedly.

theme.......... (as in "topic") Friendship was the theme for the program.

turn .... (as in "change" or "became") The trees turned yellow.

type .... (as in "favorite" or "kind") He's not my type.

various......... (as in "different" or "diverse") He saw various fish in the water.

whole.......... (as in "all") The whole class got sick.

youth .... (as in "young" or "children") The youth of our country; He belongs to a youth group.

<u>INITI</u> sign plus lipsynch

character . . . . (as in "**r**ole")
chance . . . . (as in "happen")
civilization . . . . . (as in "advance" plus "people" sign) also can use "future" or "past," sign with "group" + "people"
degree . . . . (as in "temperature")
district . . . . (as in "**a**rea")
economic . . . . . . (as in "money")
education . . . . . . (spell "ed" as in "teach")
environment . . . . (RH "e" circles LH index)
fund . . . . ("f" on palm as in "money")
grammar . . . . (as in "language")
human . . . . (as in "**p**hysical" or "**p**erson")
illustrate . . . . (as in "**s**how" or "**e**xample")
logical . . . . (as in "think")
material . . . . (as in "thing" or "**e**quipment") go from fingerspelled position to open hand, palm up
model . . . . (as in "show")
official . . . . (as in "authority") He's an official; (as in "for sure") It's official now, also PARA "definite"
opinion . . . . (as in "think")
period . . . . (as in "**t**ime") "p" to palm
physical . . . . (as in "body")
policy . . . . (as in "first" or "priority"); (as in "regulation") "p" down palm
scenes . . . . (as in "clean," using the "s" handshape) "s" on palm, l to r
usually . . . . (as in "normally")

<u>COMBO</u> sign plus lipsynch

choir . . . . "sing" + "group" or "c" hand as you make "sing" sign
fellow . . . . "connect" + "person"
input . . . . "information" + "get" or for "feedback" (f's alternate back and forth as in "communication," one palm in, the other out)
output . . . . "information" + offer"
popular . . . . (claw hand circles index)
population . . . . . "people" + "number"
product . . . . "**p**roduce" + "thing"
term . . . . "time" + "limit"
thrifty or frugal . "wise" + "money" + "person" or "careful"
throughout . . . . . "through" + "entire"

<u>PICTO</u> like sign plus lipsynch

draperies . . . . use the "4" handshape both hands move downward

RECOMMENDED SIGN LANGUAGE TEXTS AND DICTIONARIES

Cokely, Dennis, and Charlotte Baker, **American Sign Language: A Student Text** (3 vols.); **A Teacher's Resource Text** (2 vols.). Silver Spring, Maryland: T.J. Publishers, 1980.

Humphries, Tom, Carol Padden, and Terrence J. O'Rourke, **A Basic Course in American Sign Language**. Silver Spring, Maryland: T.J. Publishers, 1980.

Humphries, Tom, and Carol Padden, **Learning American Sign Language.** Englewood Cliffs, New Jersey: Prentice-Hall, 1992.

Madsen, Willard, **Conversational Sign Language II: An Intermediate-Advanced Manual**. Silver Spring, Maryland: NAD, 1972.

Riekehof, Lottie, **The Joy of Signing**. Springfield, Missouri: Gospel Publishing House, 1987.

Shroyer, Edgar H., **Signs of the Times**. Washington, D.C.: Clerc Books, Gallaudet University Press, 1991. (Fifth printing)

Smith, Cheri, Ella Mae Lentz, and Ken Mikos, **Signing Naturally I, II and Videotapes**. Vista American Sign Language Series. San Diego: DawnSignPress, 1988.

Stedt. J.D. and Donald F. Moores, **American Sign Language & Signed English Systems: An Historical Perspective and Current Realities**. H. Bornstein, editor. **Manual Communication in American Education**, Washington, D.C.: Gallaudet University Press, 1990.

Sternberg, Martin L.A., **American Sign Language: A Comprehensive Dictionary**, New York: Harper Collins Publishers, 1981.

REFERENCES

Anthony, D. **Signing Essential English.** Anaheim, California: Anaheim School District, 1971.

Bellugi, U. and Newkirk, D. "Formal Devices for Creating New Signs in ASL." **First National Symposium on Sign Language Research and Teaching.** Ed. W. Stokoe. Silver Spring, Maryland: National Association of the Deaf, 1980. 39-80

Bornstein, H. "A Description of Some Current Sign Systems Designed to Represent English." *American Annals of the Deaf*, 118 (1973): 454-463.

Bragg, B. **Lessons in Laughter.** Washington, D.C.: Gallaudet University Press, 1989.

Bragg, B. "Communication and the Deaf Community." **Communication Issues Among Deaf People.** Ed. M. Garretson. Silver Spring, Maryland: National Association of the Deaf, 1990. 9.

Cornett, R.O. "Cued Speech." *American Annals of the Deaf*, 112 (1967): 3-13.

Cornett, R.O. "In Answer to Dr. Moores." *American Annals of the Deaf,* 114 (1969): 27-29.

Corson, Harvey. J. **Comparing Deaf Children of Oral Deaf Parents and Deaf Parents using Manual Communication with Deaf Children of Hearing Parents on Academic, Social, and Communicative Functioning.** Cincinnati, Ohio: Unpublished doctoral dissertation, Univeristy of Cincinnati.

Corson, H. J. "Deaf Studies: A Framework for Learning and Teaching." Keynote Address by Harvey Jay Corson, Ed.D., Provost, Gallaudet University, Washington, D.C. at Deaf Studies for Educators National Conference, Dallas, Texas, March 7-10, 1991.

Eastman, G. **From Mime to Sign.** Silver Spring, Maryland: T.J. Publishers, 1989.

Gustason, G.; Pfezinger, D., and Swalkow, E. **Signing Exact English.** Rossmoore, California: Modern Signs Press, 1972.

Klima, E., and Bellugi, U. **The Signs of Language.** Cambridge, Massachuestts: Harvard University Press, 1979.

Lucas, C. **The Sociolinguistics of the Deaf Community.** San Diego, California: Academic Press, Inc., 1989.

Lucas, C. **Sign Language Research.** Washington, D.C.: Gallaudet University Press, 1990.

Olson, J. "Project IDEA." *American Annals of the Deaf*, 134-35 (1989): 338-340.

Olson, J. "The Garden Cafe." *American Annals of the Deaf*, 137-3 (1992): 283-287.

Olson, J. **Deaf Commmunities of the World.** Salem, Oregon: Bridge Publishing, 1994.

Quigley, S. **The Influence of Fingerspelling on the Development of Language, Communication and Educational Achievement of Deaf Children.** Urbana: University of Illinois, 1969.

Riekehof, Lottie. **The Joy of Signing.** Gospel Publishing House, Springfield, Missouri, 1987.

Scouten, E. **A Re-evaluation of the Rochester Method.** Rochester, New York: Rochester School for the Deaf, 1942.

Stedt, J.D., and Moores, D.F. **American Sign Language & Signed English Systems: An Historical Perspective and Current Realities.** H. Bornstein (Editor), **Manual Communication in American Education.** Washington, D.C.: Gallaudet University Press, 1990., pp. 6-34.

Sternberg, M.L.A. **American Sign Language: A Comprehensive Dictionary.** New York: Harper Collins Publishers, 1981.

Stokoe, W. "Sign Language Structure." *Studies in Linguistics*, Linstok Press Occasional Paper No. 8, 1958.

Van Cleve, J. V., Editor in Chief, **Gallaudet Encyclopedia of Deaf People and Deafness.** New York: McGraw-Hill, Volume 2, p. 197.

Voelker, C. "The One-Thousand Most Frequently Spoken Words," *Quarterly Journal of Speech*, April, 1942.

Like what you've been reading?
Want to order a copy for yourself, or an extra for a friend?

Meeting Halfway in American Sign Language

A Common Ground for Effective Communication
Among Deaf and Hearing People

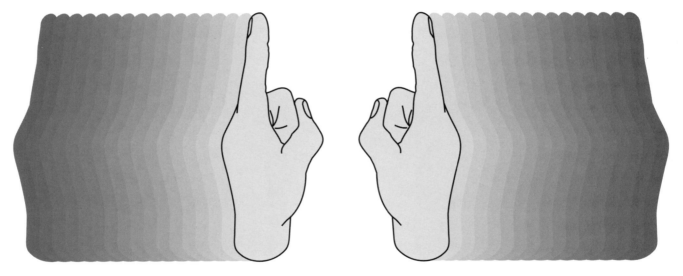

Single copy: $39.95 (plus $2.00 shipping and handling).*

Outside U.S.: $42.95 plus $3.00 shipping and handling (U.S. funds only). *New York residents, please add 8% sales tax.
Send check or money order with name, address, and phone/fax number to: MEETING HALFWAY,
c/o DEAF LIFE Press, Box 23380, Rochester, New York 14692-3380. FAX: (716) 328-6720.

Special quantity discounts (10 or more copies) are available. Contact us for details.
Orders take 2 to 6 weeks for delivery.
Handling time, prices, postage, etc., subject to change without notice.

Also available from DEAF LIFE Press

WHAT IS DEAF CULTURE?

"What is Deaf Culture? Has anyone studied it from a sociological perspective?"

"*How* did Alexander Graham Bell almost succeed in wiping out Deaf Culture?"

At the airport, I was approached by a Deaf person selling manual-alphabet cards. Should I buy one?

2nd Edition

For Hearing People ONLY

Answers To Some of the Most Commonly Asked Questions About the Deaf Community, its Culture, and the "Deaf Reality"

MATTHEW S. MOORE & LINDA LEVITAN
With a foreword by Harlan Lane

#1 best-selling book in the Deaf community

Paperback $19.95
ISBN 0-9634016-1-0

2nd Edition

For Hearing People ONLY

Answers To Some of the Most Commonly Asked Questions About the Deaf Community, its Culture, and the "Deaf Reality"

S. MOORE & LINDA LEVITAN
foreword by Harlan Lane

Hardcover $35.00
Limited Edition—2,500
ISBN 0-9634016-2-9

Deaf people: Tired of having to answer the same old questions? Tired of having to explain your culture over and over again to hearing people?

Hearing people: Need a "quick fix" for your questions about the Deaf community? Ever wished there was an enjoyable laypeople's handbook on Deaf Studies?

Here's a solution! In one handy volume, in a Q/A format, are concise answers to some of the most commonly asked questions about the Deaf community, its culture, sign language, and communication. Written in a simple, clear, non-technical style for those without any prior background. All 60 chapters of the popular "For Hearing People Only" feature from the first 5 years of **DEAF LIFE** are included—newly revised, expanded, and illustrated. 336 pages.

Single-copy orders:
Paperback—$19.95 (U.S.)/$22.95 (outside U.S.)
plus $2.00 p/h.*
Hardcover—$35.00 (U.S.)/$38.00 (outside U.S.)
plus $2.00 p/h.*
*New York residents, please add 8% sales tax.
Send check or money order with name, address, and phone/fax number to:
**HPO Book, c/o MSM Productions, Ltd.
Box 23380, Rochester, New York 14692-3380.
FAX: (716) 328-6720.**

Special quantity discounts (10 or more copies) are available. Contact us for details.
Orders take 2 to 6 weeks for delivery.
Handling time, prices, postage, etc., subject to change without notice.